A Study Of

Salvation,

Eternal Life,

And How To Obtain It

By Carey W Scott

Forward

As with any spiritual subject, the Bible is the best source to turn to. Often times, the Bible is its own best commentary. The more we stay away from the teachings of men, the better chance we will learn from God what He wants us to do.

While I may make mistakes because I am not perfect, I know and believe that God does not make mistakes, and I trust the Holy Spirit has brought to us the inspired inerrant word of God. Therefore I have confidence that as long as I present God's word, my teaching will be in accordance with God's will. We should all strive and seek to do the same.

Why do I feel we need another book? There are so many books dealing with religious and spiritual matters in the world already. Well, I do believe that much misinformation has been presented and people need to understand what salvation is all about. I do believe if we understand it, we can appreciate it. Such appreciation is lacking so much in the religious world today. I will also point out that the words used to describe eternal salvation have undergone an evolution that people need to be aware of. Of course, my main reason is to speak the truth because much false teaching has been taught on this subject. These false teachers have caused many people to lose their souls forever.

I do not suggest that I will be able to cover this subject completely. The subject itself has many variations of its own. I realize that some people will appreciate this book, and I know that many people will never read it, nor will they have an interest in this subject.

What I have learned over many years is the fact that there are no easy solutions. Yet I also realize that each person has the ability to take the solutions given to us by God and apply them which will result in eternal salvation. We know that many people teach that the Bible is too difficult to understand. I reject such a statement. It is only difficult if one wants it to be and if they are not willing to accept their accountability before God.

As I will say several times in this book; salvation takes a lifetime to achieve. I only hope that I can encourage readers to apply the knowledge of God to their lives so that they can obtain eternal life.

The quotations in this book are primarily from the King James Version. If other versions are used, they will be indicated in parenthesis.

A study Of Salvation, Eternal Life, And How To Obtain It

Introduction

In the world that we live in, a fast paced society is ruling our lives. We have our microwave ovens, convenience stores, self-serve gas stations, and of course our fast food restaurants. Even at places that are not considered fast food, they had better get the food to the customer fast or they lose customers. Instead of mailing a letter, we send it overnight, fax it, or send it across the computer via phone lines or satellite. Our cars are faster. Our computers need to be replaced every so often because the new models are faster. For most people and businesses, when you want something, you want it now.

As a result of this fast paced philosophy that we have developed, we are constantly trying to be more efficient, effective, and productive. All of this is for the purpose of getting the job done right the first time without having to do it over. Thus leaving us time to do those things which we would enjoy doing. We are always looking for short-cuts, better, faster ways to do things. If we want to go on a leisurely vacation, we rush to the airport to get to our destination real fast so that we can have time to do more (or less) things.

Because of the mentality of our society, most religions are trying to accommodate man in the "faith" field. People try to find a quick easy simple way to accomplish something without having to do the hard work or use some elbow-grease. Rather than mow your lawn, you pay someone to do it for you. This mentality has been putting pressure on the religions of today, and many religions are trying to comply in order to help these people find quick, easy, safe ways to provide salvation. However, as we study, there are no quick fixes in this business of saving souls.

While men may teach their precepts that one can be saved by faith only, we are going to let the Bible teach us that while faith is certainly an important component of our salvation; it is not the only component of our salvation. We will show that faith coupled with other things is what eventually brings salvation to us. No one thing can stand alone that produces salvation. In fact, most of the things we will discuss work together combining our faith and obedience to God's grace and commandments. When we get to the point where we are learning more each day about the things necessary for us to be saved, we find that we still have more things that we can do to insure our soul's salvation.

As our title suggest, we are dealing with eternal salvation and how to obtain it. Our first objective is to view the word "salvation" as it is used in the scripture. We will see how the word is used in various ways and try to understand how the writers of the bible understood this word. We will also look at the word "eternal" which also has some interesting understandings associated with it. As we go through the Bible we will notice a gradual change in the meaning of the words. This can be described as an evolution of the language. Any living language has words that for one culture might mean one thing, and a following generation might take the same word to mean something entirely different. Some words of our English language have evolved into complete opposites in some cases.

In all of this we should learn that the original meaning of Salvation has evolved over the many years. We see it in the Old Testament where most of the time, the use of the word deals with things in the physical world. As we get into the prophecy writings, there begins to be a new meaning to the concept of salvation. Once we get to the New Testament, we will find that there is now a spiritual application of the use of the word. Just because the word takes on a spiritual application does not mean that the physical is to be ignored. Quite the contrary; what we do and how we live in the physical realm does have bearing upon our soul's eternal destination.

The first chapter will be dealing with the historical writings of scripture. In these instances, the salvation that is derived is in the deliverance from the oppression of enemies, whether physical or natural.

The next chapter will be dealing with the word used in the poetry writings. It carries a dual meaning in poetry, for sometimes it is referring to deliverance from enemies, and sometimes it carries the thought of acquiring inner peace through a close kindred relationship with God.

The next chapter after that will be dealing with the books of prophecy. In these books, the word carries the above meanings along with the future promise of salvation. That future promise of salvation is something that the Old Testament writers did not understand (1 Peter 1:10-12). This was the mystery that was not made known until the establishment of the Church in the New Testament or Christian age.

The next chapter will be dealing with the Christ and His church. The teaching of the New Testament has a general theme (even though there are many themes) of eternal life; a.k.a. eternal salvation. We should see the meaning of the word in several ways. A few times the word has a meaning of deliverance and protection. Several times the word is used to describe an inner peace with God. But once we get through the gospels, we will find that the meaning of the word is usually describing the afterlife for our soul. Our souls are eternal, and must abide somewhere. We know there are only two possible destinies for our soul; heaven or hell.

We will also look at the words translated in the Hebrew and Greek languages for "eternal" and see how they are used. We will learn that the concept of eternal life (as we know it) was foreign to those of the Old Testament times, yet through prophecy, they knew that someday, somehow, they could become eternal (like God). The concept of eternal comes to mankind in the teachings about the kingdom of God. It is through the gospel that life and immortality are brought to light (2 Timothy 1:10).

We will also deal with the idea that in the New Testament there are three types of salvation. There is the salvation from past sins which happens when a person of faith obeys from the heart the doctrine of Christ and obeys the commands and teachings of Christ. We also learn of a salvation of present sins which happens when we confess our sins before God (and sometimes man) and repent to make the effort to not continue in sin. Finally the third use of the word deals with the ultimate victory of spending eternity in heaven with God and Jesus forever. Like I said in the introduction, people misunderstand the meaning of words and get them confused. Such is the case when one hears of being saved from our past sins, yet thinking it automatically gives us a life in heaven. No, that is wrong. We have to continue growing in God's grace and knowledge for the rest of our life to receive the eternal life in heaven.

Our last chapter will be the most extensive. We are going to look at many thoughts provided by the scriptures that have a bearing upon our soul's condition. At first thought you may think that some things are not as important as other things. Yet realizing that God put it in the Bible is enough reason to treat it as important. There will be a challenge to each reader to examine their self (2 Corinthians 13:5) to see if they measure up to the standard God has given all of us. That will be the most challenging thing for all of us as we begin to learn that obtaining salvation takes a lifetime to acquire the things we need to do to please God. The new Christian (babe in Christ) may feel overwhelmed when first looking at the list, and it is designed to give them goals that they are to grow in. Many seasoned Christians will see that they have accomplished many of these things in their life, but there is always room to grow. Anyone who says they have done enough is wrong, and they may not get to heaven.

Another problem in our world today is the failure to understand words alike. What one person may understand by a word could be completely different from the understanding of another person. This subject about Salvation can be viewed from many different perspectives. Our hope is to provide an understanding of the word, and the concept behind the word and to understand it from a Biblical perspective. We will use God's words to explain this subject.

This book is written in hopes that someone will get a clearer understanding of what Salvation is all about. The ultimate goal is to help people get to heaven, and understanding what salvation is and what it does is vital to getting there. We will not examine every scripture with the word "Salvation" or the word "eternal". But the verses we will use should teach us valuable lessons about our salvation.

Salvation In Old Testament Historical Writings

This section deals with the Hebrew word found in the Hebrew texts concerning salvation.

Yshuwah;(3444) help, deliverance, salvation, victory, welfare. This word is a feminine passive participle derived from the word Yasha (3467) which means "to be open wide or free". In the abstract sense, it is something saved or delivered. If one is fortunate enough to find himself in that condition, he is in good health and enjoys prosperity. It connotes the idea of being comfortable, having no problems. The act of giving aid to the distressed produces deliverance and safety. The source of this salvation comes from outside the situation of oppression. A savior may rescue people from national or individual emergencies, enemies, natural catastrophes, plagues, famine, or sickness. At first, the term was used in an ordinary sense, but later, both in the O.T. and the N.T., the term acquired a very strong spiritual meaning. Jehovah is the God of our salvation. Salvation is associated with the forgiveness of sin. Satan must be defeated and we must be delivered from him and his power. *(Spiros Zodhaites, Hebrew/Greek Key study Bible pg 1733).*

From the definition above, we can understand how the word is used in scripture.

Let us review several scriptures and see how this progresses through time.

Genesis 49:18 "I have waited for Thy <u>salvation</u>, O LORD".
This is uttered in the context of Jacob telling his sons what was to come about in future days. This was a sort of family prophecy. Some of which we can find came true.

Exodus 14:13 "And Moses said unto the people, Fear ye not, stand still, and see the <u>salvation</u> of the LORD, which He will show to you today: for the Egyptians whom ye have seen today, ye shall see them again no more forever".
The people are all complaining because they are blocked by the Red Sea, and Pharaoh's army is fast approaching. Moses tells them to see the event which will bring about their deliverance. This story of their deliverance was to be passed on to subsequent generations throughout their history as a people. God caused the Red Sea to divide and the people were allowed safety and deliverance on the other side. This also meant the destruction of Pharaoh's army, and the people no longer had to fear them.

Exodus 15:2 "The LORD is my strength and song, and He is become my <u>salvation</u>: He is my God, and I will prepare Him an habitation; my father's God, and I will exalt him".

This is part of the song of Moses, how God had delivered them from their oppressors and made them a free independent nation of people. These oppressed people have been delivered from their oppressors, and Moses reminds the people that God is the one responsible.

Deuteronomy 32:15 "But Jeshurun waxed fat, and kicked: thou art waxen fat, thou art grown thick, thou art covered with fatness; then he forsook God which made him, and lightly esteemed the Rock of his salvation".
This is another song of Moses of how Israel has treated the God of their deliverance. The people are about to enter the Promised Land and take possession of all that it offers. Yet the people are still obstinate, and headed for destruction. They should be excited and filled with joy that God has shown them favor, but they are selfish and are not satisfied with what God has done for them.

1 Samuel 2:1 "And Hannah prayed, and said, My heart rejoiceth in the LORD, mine horn is exalted in the LORD: my mouth is enlarged over mine enemies; because I rejoice in Thy salvation".
The prayer of Hannah as she brought the child, she had prayed for, to Eli, for the purpose of dedicating the child to the Lord for service. The prayer is prophetic in nature and almost mirrors many of the words of Moses as he gave warnings to the children of Israel. The prophets will describe virtually everything in this prayer as being attributable to the children of Israel. We see that in just about every case of salvation, God is the one who saves His people. He also puts conditions upon those who would receive this salvation.

1 Samuel 11:13 "And Saul said, 'There shall not a man be put to death this day: for today the LORD hath wrought salvation in Israel".
Saul warns that no more life need be taken because God had already delivered them from their enemies.

1 Samuel 14:45 "And the people said unto Saul, Shall Jonathan die, who hath wrought this great salvation in Israel? God forbid: as the LORD liveth, there shall not one hair of his head fall to the ground; for he hath wrought with God this day. So the people rescued Jonathan that he died not".
In v.24, Saul had placed the people under an oath to not eat anything until the victory had been accomplished. It is later revealed that the captain of the army responsible for the deliverance of Israel, Jonathan, had eaten some honey that he came across. Jonathan was ready to die, but the people would not allow it.

1 Samuel 19:5 "For he did put his life in His hand, and slew the Philistine, and the LORD wrought a great salvation for all Israel: thou sawest it, and didst rejoice: wherefore then wilt thou sin against innocent blood, to slay David without a cause?"
Saul had been jealous of David for quite some time. Saul commanded David to attack the Philistines, which David did, and delivered Israel from their enemy again. Once again the scripture tells us that it is God who brought deliverance from their enemies. David was just the one whom God used to accomplish this. This story also puts a focus

upon David who will be instrumental in the greater scheme of God's plan in the future.

2 Samuel 22:3 "The God of my rock; in Him will I trust: He is my shield, and the horn of my salvation, my high tower, and my refuge, my Saviour; thou savest me from violence".
David utters a prayer or psalm of thanksgiving for the deliverance that God gave him from all his enemies and from the hand of Saul. Remember that Saul tried to kill David on several occasions, but God helped David to survive.

2 Samuel 22:36 "Thou hast also given me the shield of Thy salvation: and Thy gentleness hath made me great".
This is a continuation of the psalm of thanksgiving. We see here that David feels as long as he trusts in the Lord, that the Lord will protect him and deliver him from all sorts of evil. The Lord does the same for us today.

2 Samuel 22:47 "The LORD liveth; and blessed be my rock; and exalted be the God of the rock of my salvation".
If we put our trust in God, he remains as solid as a rock in being the great deliverer that we need. We now begin to see some metaphors in use of describing God and the salvation He provides. This also brings to mind what Jesus said about the man (woman) who hears His sayings being likened to a man who builds his house upon a solid foundation of a rock (Matthew 7:24-25)

2 Samuel 22:51 "He is the tower of salvation for His king: and showeth mercy to His anointed, unto David, and to his seed for evermore".
Described as a great watchtower in which there is safety as long as the watchmen keep watch. God appointed Ezekiel as a watchman (Chapter 3:17). His job was to warn the people of the danger of turning away from God. The watchman took his position upon a high tower to see a far off distance so that if an enemy approached, the people could be summoned to arms and be ready to defend the city.

2 Samuel 23:5 "Although my house be not so with God; yet He hath made with me an everlasting covenant, ordered in all things, and sure: for this is all my salvation, and all my desire, although He make it not to grow".
This use of the word could be as it is used in the poetry verses. While David was meek and humble enough to realize he did not deserve God's blessings, he sees deliverance from enemies and calamities. David is quick to point out that God helped David through these trials. But we also see a glimpse of an inner peace by being a person in whom God was well pleased.

1 Chronicles 16:23 "Sing unto the LORD, all the earth; show forth from day to day His salvation".
This is another rendition of the praise psalm of David that is recorded in 2 Samuel 22. David gave us many psalms, David writes: "O Lord, open my lips, and my mouth will declare your praise (Psalm 51:15) (ESV)".
All Israel was commanded to let the world know that God is the great deliverer for His

people. There were times when the people of the world saw the great wonders and realized that this people had a living God and they learned to respect this God. This was always the duty of God's people to share God with the world, but so often, they failed in promoting God. The people of the world could have used the knowledge of God, and the world would have been a better place. The problem was that God's people did not live up to His standards, and they certainly did not share what great things God had done for them.

1 Chronicles 16:35 "And say ye, Save us, O God of our salvation, and gather us together, and deliver us from the heathen, that we may give thanks to Thy holy name, and glory in Thy praise".
This is part of a prayer included in the psalm which invokes upon God His continued blessings and deliverance, which is dependent upon the people's faithfulness. You see that they could have been saved, but they chose to reject their God.

2 Chronicles 6:41 "Now therefore arise, O LORD God, into Thy resting place, Thou, and the ark of Thy strength: let Thy priests, O LORD God, be clothed with salvation, and let Thy saints rejoice in goodness".
This is a prayer of Solomon in which he suggests that the priest be delivered from oppression and plagues in order to carry out their duties as priest of the Most High God. Solomon sets an example that all of God's people should pray for their spiritual leaders at all times. Not only should they pray for them, but they should show their support as these men do what they try to do for the Master.

2 Chronicles 20:17 "Ye shall not need to fight in this battle: set yourselves, stand ye still, and see the salvation of the LORD with you, O Judah and Jerusalem: fear not, nor be dismayed; tomorrow go out against them: for the LORD will be with you".
After Jehoshaphat had prayed to God, a Levite priest was prompted to speak on behalf of God, telling them to let God fight their battles. As the people went out on the morrow, they found that their enemies had been defeated and killed themselves. Thus Israel was spared and God was glorified for protecting and delivering His people.

As you can see, most of these verses speak of salvation as a deliverance from their enemies. God promised them through Moses that if they would obey Him, He would see to their welfare (Leviticus 26 and Deuteronomy 28).

Salvation In The Old Testament Poetry Writings

This section will deal with the use of the Hebrew word Yshuwah, which is translated "salvation". We take these from the writings of poetry from the Old Testament. For a proper description of this word, see the beginning of the historical writings in the beginning of the previous chapter.

We will notice that the word seems to gradually progress between deliverance from enemies and catastrophes into a type of spiritual (individual) deliverance. Though the people of the Old Testament times did not understand the concept of eternal life, they did recognize that God was great and merciful. They understood that as long as they tried to be faithful, that God would bless them accordingly. After all, this is what God had promised through Moses. By having peace, prosperity, and health, the people would realize that God was in charge and responsible for their glory. As the people turned their back on God, problems would come upon them.

We sometimes see in this poetry the idea that the individual is responsible to God even though the nation may be transgressing God's laws. The individual can still be blessed, even if the rest of the nation is suffering.

Let us look at these passages of poetry and see how the word is used.

Job 13:16 "He also shall be my salvation: for an hypocrite shall not come before Him". Job had just stated the famous quote; "Though He slay me, I will hope in Him". Because Job had placed his trust in the Lord, his faith would bring about deliverance from his trials. We find in the last chapter that God rewarded the faith of Job greatly.

Psalm 3:8 "Salvation belongeth unto the LORD: thy blessing is upon Thy people. *Selah*".
Who else has the capability to deliver the people? Who else can provide this salvation? God offers this salvation because of His love for us and His expression of mercy found in His grace.

Psalm 9:14 "That I may show forth all Thy praise in the gates of the daughter of Zion: I will rejoice in Thy salvation".
David makes the request to God to deliver him from his enemies. As a result, David promises to declare unto the people and all peoples the great deliverance that his God can provide. Remember that only God can provide such salvation. No governments, powers, rulers, nor leaders of men can bring about this kind of salvation. Some may receive a form of freedom, but it pales in comparison of what God offers.

Psalm 13:5 "But I have trusted in Thy mercy; my heart shall rejoice in Thy salvation".
David in this psalm has asked God to answer his prayer. He offers this reason for

accepting the salvation of God; his trust.

Psalm 14:7 "Oh that the salvation of Israel were come out of Zion! when the LORD bringeth back the captivity of His people, Jacob shall rejoice, and Israel shall be glad". The salvation of Israel will come from the God that makes His physical home in Zion (symbolic as God is everywhere). The captivity seems to reflect the constant attacks by the wicked upon God's people. As we will read in the prophecy writings, the people who return from captivity will be restored to God's service because God is the one who delivered them.

Psalm 18:2 "The LORD is my rock, and my fortress, and my deliverer; my God, my strength, in whom I will trust; my buckler, and the horn of my salvation, and my high tower".
This is the Psalm of thanksgiving as recorded in 2 Samuel 22 and 1 Chronicles 16. The Lord had provided salvation for David from his enemies. The phrase "horn" is usually associated with power. So the "power of my salvation" fits and is attributed to God who is also described as a solid rock, fortress, deliverer (which is kind of redundant in this verse), strength, buckler (small round shield used in warfare), and high tower (the taller the better). In other words, David can think of no one better than God for his protection.

Psalm 18:35 "Thou hast also given me the shield of Thy salvation: and Thy right hand hath holden me up, and Thy gentleness hath made me great".
David says that this salvation is like a shield. David acknowledges that he is powerless to do anything for good without God being there to hold him up. The "right" hand is usually portrayed as the stronger hand, thus we have God using His strength to uphold David through various trials. Even David says that any greatness directed towards him most certainly has to be extended to Almighty God. Though David was a king, and had all sorts of power, David gave the glory and greatness to God. Notice also that David speaks of God's gentleness that has made David great. Up to this point, we see God portrayed as a fierce controller over mankind. We begin to see a gentle side of God who has compassion and care for His people, and this is leading up to the giving of His Son.

Psalm 18:46 "The LORD liveth; and blessed be my rock; and let the God of my salvation be exalted".
This is also recorded in 2 Samuel 22:47. Even though this is mentioned in our history section, we have to realize that a lot of the poetry happened during the age of history. This is a continuation of the previous thought. The God who provides salvation must be exalted. Everything we do should be to His glory. Compare this to 1 Peter 4:11. This is one of those verses that all Christians should commit to memory and live like they mean what it says.

Psalm 20:5 "We will rejoice in Thy salvation, and in the name of our God we will set up our banners: the LORD fulfil all thy petitions".
Some other versions use the word "victory" in place of "salvation". God must receive the credit for our victories. We are to rejoice that God has provided salvation. That rejoicing

needs to be seen through our faithful obedience and the praise we offer to God. This is one of those things in which we can declare to all mankind just how great and awesome our God really is. We also see that we can trust that God answers our prayers when we have put our trust in Him.

Psalm 21:1 *"To the chief Musician, A Psalm of David.* The king shall joy in Thy strength, O LORD; and in Thy <u>salvation</u> how greatly shall he rejoice!
All those in power must recognize that there is a greater power. In fact they would not be in power had God not willed it so. These are the thoughts Daniel (Chapter two) used when explaining to Nebuchadnezzar how God puts kings and rulers into power. Everyone should be able to rejoice when they know God has provided salvation for them.

Psalm 21:5 "His glory is great in Thy <u>salvation</u>: honour and majesty hast thou laid upon him".
Both of these passages are describing the triumph of King David. As David gives God the glory He deserves. David also attributes recognition to God for all of his own accomplishments. David had received the honor and majesty in the physical realm, and attributes such to God's blessings.

Psalm 24:5 "He shall receive the blessing from the LORD, and righteousness from the God of his <u>salvation</u>.
This psalm is a prophetic utterance describing who may come into the presence of God. Only the one with clean hands and a pure heart may enter that presence. Jesus was the only one who ever approached God with clean hands and a pure heart. But we should consider it a great blessing that God has granted to us a way to cleanse ourselves. Anybody can attempt to come to God with a good heart, but that is only part of the formula. One must be cleansed of sin before one can come into the presence of God. We learn in Acts 22:16 that baptism is that act of obedience which washes away our sins, as we call upon the Lord in faith. There is no salvation without baptism into Christ in the age we are now in.

Psalm 25:5 "Lead me in Thy truth, and teach me: for Thou art the God of my <u>salvation</u>; on Thee do I wait all the day".
Though we can constantly repeat that salvation is deliverance, we begin to see in the writings of David that salvation is also self-realized within one's own soul. Paul describes this as "the peace which surpasses all understanding"(Philippians 4:7). This comes about when we receive instruction from the Lord. How do we receive such instruction? It comes to us through His word; the Bible. We see the phrase to wait all the day. We should be thirsty for the words of righteousness. We should hunger and thirst for such (Matthew 5:6). When we make it our daily goal to learn from God, He will teach us the way that leads to salvation.

Psalm 27:1 *"A Psalm of David.* The LORD is my light and my <u>salvation</u>; whom shall I fear? The LORD is the strength of my life; of whom shall I be afraid?
With God as our shield, defender, and protector, who can possibly mount a successful

attack against us? The answer is no one. Not even Satan has the power to conquer us. If we give in to temptation so as to be lost, we cannot blame Satan, we can only blame ourselves. See James 1:13-15 where we all fall short of God.

Psalm 27:9 "Hide not Thy face far from me; put not Thy servant away in anger: Thou hast been my help; leave me not, neither forsake me, O God of my salvation".
It is as if David is saying; "Lord, don't leave me, you are my protection". Do not we also hope that God is near when we need Him? Of course God is always near, yet sometimes we forget that fact. It is those times we forget God is near that we tend to do naughty things. When we think about it, we deserve the punishment God has in store for the wicked. But we must also thank God for helping us find the pathway that will lead us to salvation.

Psalm 35:3 "Draw out also the spear, and stop the way against them that persecute me: say unto my soul, I am thy salvation".
We might ask God to impress our memory banks with the thought that God is our deliverer. This is so that we will not forget who to turn to when we cannot handle a situation by ourselves. Remind us O Lord that you are the one who fights our battles for us.

Psalm 35:9 "And my soul shall be joyful in the LORD: it shall rejoice in His salvation".
The Lord does offer salvation, and our hearts should be joyful when we realize that God has blessed us and saved us from danger. We should also be reminded that keeping God's word is necessary also. Yes, God has provided His grace, but it is conditional upon our obedience to His word.

Psalm 37:39 "But the salvation of the righteous is of the LORD: He is their strength in the time of trouble".
Salvation can come from no other source than Almighty God. Notice also, that salvation is for the righteous. Whenever we are tempted, we must call upon God to see us through so that we do not fall into temptation. It is by knowing that God is "strong to deliver" that should motivate us to remain faithful to Him.

Psalm 38:22 "Make haste to help me, O Lord my salvation".
Sometimes we get impatient and want things right now. There are times when so much of the world begins to overwhelm us that we need God and we need Him right now. We need to remember when we get tempted to call upon God immediately for our deliverance. When we have such a mind to do that, we are more than likely to be able to resist the temptation presented to us. David states that the Lord is the source of his salvation.

Psalm 40:10 "I have not hid Thy righteousness within my heart; I have declared Thy faithfulness and Thy salvation: I have not concealed Thy lovingkindness and Thy truth from the great congregation".
David led his people in the ways of God. The people were faithful because David proclaimed the greatness of Jehovah God. Also consider that it is a selfish thing to not

share God with those who need Him. God had blessed David so much, that he wanted the whole world to know how great and awesome God really is. We should not conceal our faith in the world we live in. You might think that you can escape persecution by keeping your faith hidden from your friends and neighbors; but you are doing them a disservice by not sharing God and His mercy to them. You needed to learn about God and His salvation; they need to learn about Him also,

Psalm 40:16 "Let all those that seek Thee rejoice and be glad in Thee: let such as love Thy salvation say continually, The LORD be magnified".
Notice that salvation has come across the span from being just a deliverance from physical problems into a spiritual type of trust placed in the great Deliverer of us all. Also, we see that if we love the salvation God has given to us, we are to praise God and magnify Him. To magnify something is to make it appear larger. Of course, no matter how much larger, powerful, loving and greater we portray our God; He excels even our grandest imaginations of Him.

Psalm 50:23 "Whoso offereth praise glorifieth me: and to him that ordereth his conversation aright will I show the salvation of God".
Here, David tells his people that anyone who will not follow God is an enemy of the state. David also seems to be seeking recognition that he is the King and should be honored for such. Upon people respecting the King, the King will tell the people about how great God is. This phrase "ordereth his conversation aright" is speaking of living a righteous lifestyle. Yes, we need to follow God's guidelines so as to be considered righteous in His sight.

Psalm 51:12 "Restore unto me the joy of Thy salvation; and uphold me with Thy free spirit".
This is the speaking of the repentance that David shows after the child dies from the adulterous relationship with Bathsheba. David has sinned before God, and knows that God is not happy with him. David misses the joy of being blessed by God because he realizes that it is his own actions that put him in this condition. Only after contrite repentance, can one expect to see the salvation of the Lord. This is where the confidence in one's own heart declares in their mind that they are righteous in the sight of God.

Psalm 51:14 "Deliver me from bloodguiltiness, O God, Thou God of my salvation: and my tongue shall sing aloud of Thy righteousness".
David says to God; "show me forgiveness, and I will praise your Holy Name to everyone". Also note that only God can forgive sins. No person on earth has such power to forgive sins. Remember that Jesus forgave someone their sins, and the spiritual leaders accused Him of blasphemy, as they said "only God can forgive sins" (Mark 2:2-12). Later Jesus would be shown to be God, Who is able to forgive sins.

Psalm 53:6 "Oh that the salvation of Israel were come out of Zion! When God bringeth back the captivity of His people, Jacob shall rejoice, and Israel shall be glad".
This is a repeat of Psalms 14:7. Notice that the nation of Israel is under consideration

by the psalmist. Often times, David spoke of his own salvation, and most salvation conversation is concerning the individual. But there are times when salvation for a nation is spoken of. This is one of those times.

Psalm 62:1 "*To the chief Musician, to Jeduthun, A Psalm of David. Truly my soul waiteth upon God: from Him cometh my* salvation".
Where else can our salvation come from? When we see the word "wait", it does not necessarily mean to stand around idle until God does something. We use this word in our culture which means to see to one's needs. Think of a waiter or waitress. Their job is to "wait" on you. We understand this means to provide you with what you want, when you want it, and make sure you do not have to ask for anything like refills or silverware. What kind of "service" are you doing for God?

Psalm 62:2 "He only is my rock and my salvation; He is my defense; I shall not be greatly moved".
God is the only one who has the strength to provide salvation. None other can effectively offer salvation. When the preacher offers salvation, he does so at the command of God, and is commissioned to only speak the truth of God's word (1 Peter 4:11). Also, when we trust in God, no force should be able to sway us away from Him.

Psalm 62:7 "In God is my salvation and my glory: the rock of my strength, and my refuge, is in God".
If anyone is to receive blessings, they will originate from God. God provides all things for us and in Him, all things are kept together. In God only, can we (should we) put our trust. When we have God on our side, we are on the winning team. There should be some excitement from that thought and a sense of pride (not too much) should come over us. God is my glory, and we should all look forward to sharing that glory with Him in eternity.

Psalm 65:5 "By terrible things in righteousness wilt Thou answer us, O God of our salvation; who art the confidence of all the ends of the earth, and of them that are afar off upon the sea":
The NASB reads: By awesome deeds, Thou dost answer us in righteousness, O God of our salvation. Thou who are the trust of all the ends of the earth and of the farthest sea;"
Everything God does is to be considered awesome. Of course they lived in a time where God used His power to show His greatness. Whatever God does to show His righteousness is going to be great. Perhaps sending His Son to this earth because of His love for mankind (John 3:16)? No matter where we are, God is there (Psalm 139).

Psalm 68:19 "Blessed be the Lord, who daily loadeth us with benefits, even the God of our salvation. *Selah*".
We probably do not ever consider that God does load us with blessings. Perhaps we are just too blind to see. His blessings are all around us. Any day that you wake up with God in your life, it becomes a blessing to you. But when you wake up and forget your God, trouble in many forms may come upon you. So wake up every day and bless the God of heaven so that you in turn can receive blessings from Him.

Psalm 68:20 "He that is our God is the God of salvation; and unto God the Lord belong the issues from death".
God blesses us beyond our comprehension and has control over our lives and our death. When we put our trust in the Lord, and join with others who do the same, there are rich blessings from such fellowship. We get to share love, compassion, joy, and many other blessings. In a way there is also a blessing in receiving discipline and chastisement from our brethren (Hebrews 12:5-13).

Psalm 69:13 "But as for me, my prayer is unto thee, O LORD, in an acceptable time: O God, in the multitude of Thy mercy hear me, in the truth of Thy salvation".
Here, David places a relationship between truth and salvation. They are inseparable and go together. You cannot have one without the other. Any time is an acceptable time to pray to God, and we are encouraged to "pray without ceasing" (1 Thessalonians 5:17). Also note that we must pray to the right God. David had many gods to choose from in his day, but he chose the God of heaven to pray to. We should also.

Psalm 69:29 "But I am poor and sorrowful: let Thy salvation, O God, set me up on high".
Humility is also required for us to receive this salvation. Jesus and Peter spoke of those who shall be first would be last, and those who shall be last, would be first. The psalmist has the attitude that we all should have. We should say "I am not great until you make me great. We know from scripture that one day God will set us up on high, but that will only happen at the end of our lives, not before.

Psalm 71:15 "My mouth shall show forth Thy righteousness and Thy salvation all the day; for I know not the numbers thereof".
Are we limited to just how many times we can tell people about God and the salvation He offers? No, we are not! Notice also that righteousness and salvation go together just like truth and salvation go together as noted back in Psalm 69:13.

Psalm 74:12 "For God is my King of old, working salvation in the midst of the earth".
There are so many different gods of this world and it seems everyone has their own concept of God. When dealing with doctrinal matters, you might hear one say something like: "Well, my God would not do that". Notice that the psalmist considered God as "my King of old". God has been around much longer than the earth. In fact, He has been the King of the earth since before the earth was formed. Also note that the great God King of the earth has been working salvation throughout the whole earth. God has been working to provide salvation since mankind first needed to be saved.

Psalm 78:22 "Because they believed not in God, and trusted not in His salvation".
There are going to be people who reject God. There is no sanity in such actions but they do it anyway. There will be some who claim to believe in God, but do not put their trust in Him or His offer of salvation. This is human nature to try to do things on your own. When it comes to our soul, we cannot take care of it on our own. Thus we need to trust God in what He says to bring about our eternal salvation. We cannot merit it,

and we can do nothing to acquire it by ourselves. We need God and His formula in our lives to make that happen.

Psalm 79:9 "Help us, O God of our <u>salvation</u>, for the glory of Thy name: and deliver us, and purge away our sins, for Thy name's sake"
This psalm is attributed to Asaph. It appears to have been written in the days of Daniel, Ezra, and Nehemiah. It also is presented as a prayer of one so distraught over the destruction of Jerusalem, and the whole nation, he turns to God to restore the glory of Israel for the sake of God's name. At one time, the world recognized Jerusalem and Judah as being in the possession of a living God. With the destruction of God's territory and people, all the earth would take opportunity to impugn God. The psalmist reminds God that the sooner He returns His glory to Jerusalem and Judah, the world will respect Him once again. This prayer is very similar to the prayers of Daniel (Chapter nine) and Nehemiah (Chapter one).

Psalm 85:4 "Turn us, O God of our <u>salvation</u>, and cause Thine anger toward us to cease".
The NASV reads: "Restore us, O God of our salvation, and cause Thine indignation toward us to cease". The Psalmist (attributed to the sons of Korah) recalls how God had forgiven their sins of the past, and now they are asking God to forgive them one more time. They asked God the question in the next verse: "Wilt Thou be angry with us forever? Wilt Thou prolong Thine anger to all generations?"(NASV). We might ask ourselves just how long God will be angry with us. The answer depends upon our humble repentance, as God will forgive immediately as soon as we restore our relationship with Him.

Psalm 85:7 "Show us Thy mercy, O LORD, and grant us Thy <u>salvation</u>".
This is a continuation of the prayer mentioned previously. Everyone who is sane and recognizes God should ask for God's mercy, and ask for the salvation that God offers.

Psalm 85:9 "Surely His <u>salvation </u>is nigh them that fear Him; that glory may dwell in our land".
The deliverance of God is near them that fear Him. The fear is not one of being afraid, but is the same fear we read in Ecclesiastes 12:13. "Fear God and keep His commands, for this applies to every person" (NASV). This fear is reverence towards God. It is a reverential respect knowing that God is the one who will make the final call concerning our eternal destiny. So if we honor and respect God, His deliverance is near. Note that it says that glory will dwell in our land. We have seen throughout history when a people live to serve God, God does dwell in their land and provide great blessings to those people.

Psalm 88:1 "*A Song or Psalm for the sons of Korah, to the chief Musician upon Mahalath Leannoth, Maschil of Heman the Ezrahite.* O LORD God of my <u>salvation</u>, I have cried day and night before Thee."
We are all encouraged to pray to almighty God continuously. What better way to capture the attention of the God of this world than to call Him "Lord"? He is the Lord

that brings salvation to me. The phrase "I cried day and night" means that the psalmist has petitioned God through prayer continuously.

Psalm 89:26 "He shall cry unto me, Thou art my father, my God, and the rock of my salvation."
This is a psalm of Ethan the Ezrahite. In this psalm, the psalmist recalls all that God had done for David through his trials. This verse is what the psalmist claims David asked God. We have read several verses where God is "the rock of my salvation". Once again, emphasizing just how solid God's protection is.

Psalm 91:16 "With long life will I satisfy him, and show him my salvation."
Verse one starts with the words: "He who dwells in the shelter of the Most High will abide in the shadow of the Almighty". This whole chapter dwells on this theme. The last three verses are worth noting. God says: (14) "Because he has loved Me, therefore I will deliver him; I will set him securely on high, because he has known My name. (15) He will call upon Me, and I will answer him; I will be with him in trouble; I will rescue him, and honor him. (16) With a long life I will satisfy him, and let him behold My salvation" (NASV).

Psalm 95:1 "O come, let us sing unto the LORD: let us make a joyful noise to the rock of our salvation."
Singing is one of the methods we employ to express our emotions in our worship to God. Many Christians find enjoyment when gathered with other Christians to sing songs of praise to God. This invitation from Psalm 95 encourages all followers of God to gather and sing praises to Him. Once again, God is called the "rock of our salvation". He is so solid and sure, nothing can move Him away from us as long as we desire to be near Him. Remember that God gives us a choice, and if we choose to ask God to leave us, He will comply. God has expressed often for people to return to Him, because God has provided a way to eternal salvation. This salvation is offered to all mankind. Each person has the ability to accept the offer or reject it. What about you? Have you accepted God's offer of salvation? Have you obeyed His commandments?

Psalm 96:2 "Sing unto the LORD, bless His name; show forth His salvation from day to day."
Yes, we should sing unto the Lord. We should tell others about God and the salvation that God offers to all. Bless His name means we should extoll the greatness of God. We should be willing to tell others that God is awesome, powerful, and merciful.

Psalm 98:2 "The LORD hath made known His salvation: His righteousness hath He openly showed in the sight of the heathen. "
For the people of that day, God spoke through Moses and the prophets. God had told the people from Mount Sinai that good would come to them if they would just obey God and serve Him. Such a promise would be a true blessing. But, alas, we see from history that God's people rejected Him and did what they wanted to do. Later on in the prophetic writings, God would declare that His people would not see His salvation because of their disobedience and rebellion.

Psalm 98:3 "He hath remembered His mercy and His truth toward the house of Israel: all the ends of the earth have seen the salvation of our God."
This happened several times in the history of Israel. The people would be oppressed and would spend some time in outright rebellion to God, yet someone would come along and straighten them out. The kings of Israel were a good example of this. Some kings were evil and some were good. The evil kings would lead the people astray and the good kings would bring them back. Every time the people turned back to serving God they would prosper and be blessed. This was something the people of the other nations recognized.

Psalm 106:4 "Remember me, O LORD, with the favour that Thou bearest unto Thy people: O visit me with Thy salvation;"
It is always a good idea to pray to God for Him to remember you. Often, I think humility gets in our way and we fail to pray on our own behalf. Sure, we pray for others that we know and some we do not know. We might think that of the near seven billion people on this earth, God might get so busy that he would forget us. Well, He does not forget. Our prayer asking God to remember us is for our benefit. With such a prayer, we put into our mind a mini-revival and realize we must act according to His will in order for the Lord God to look upon us in a favorable condition.

Psalm 116:13 "I will take the cup of salvation, and call upon the name of the LORD."
Calling on the name of the Lord in the New Testament means an appeal to God. It is accompanied by obedience. Peter quoted Joel (2:28-32) on the day of Pentecost sermon where he quotes: (21) "And it shall be, that everyone who calls on the name of the Lord shall be saved" (NASV) While this statement is true, we must also consider that there is more than just this action we must do to bring about our salvation.

Psalm 118:14 "The LORD is my strength and song, and is become my salvation."
Once again the LORD is called by metaphors. Strength that indicates God is strong to save and protect. God is the one who soothes our soul and uplifts our demeanor; thus our song as we make melody in our hearts (Ephesians 5:19), and God is our salvation which means He is the source of our salvation.

Psalm 118:15 "The voice of rejoicing and salvation is in the tabernacles of the righteous: the right hand of the LORD doeth valiantly."
The righteous are those who are committed to serving God. They are the ones who take God's word and apply it to their lives. They are the ones who teach others by following God's word as the only guide to heaven. Only the righteous rejoice at the mention of God's name. Only the righteous will receive the salvation of God. And, of course, everything that God does, He does it valiantly.

Psalm 118:21 "I will praise Thee: for Thou hast heard me, and art become my salvation."
We always need to praise God because he hears our prayers. That is, if we are faithful and righteous before Him. God does not hear the prayer of those who continue in their

sins. Being able to recognize God's response to our prayers takes faith. Things may work out by themselves, but we like to think that God has a hand in bringing about a favorable solution for us. We should always take the answer to our prayers as being the will of God. When we have this kind of trust in God, we just know in our hearts that salvation is from God, and He is the source of our salvation.

Psalm 119:41 "*VAU.* Let thy mercies come also unto me, O LORD, even thy salvation, according to thy word."

Psalm 119:81 "*CAPH.* My soul fainteth for thy salvation: but I hope in thy word."

Psalm 119:123 "Mine eyes fail for thy salvation, and for the word of thy righteousness." These three verses all have one thing in common. The word of God. Yes, we know that God's mercy and grace make salvation available to us, but it is when we keep the word of God by doing His commandments that we receive such mercy and grace. Our hope for salvation is given to us through the knowledge of His word. We can fail for salvation when we take our eyes off of the goal. As Christians, we know that the goal is heaven, and we know that Jesus is standing there on the finish line waiting to welcome us home. The Hebrew writer in 12:2 instructs us to keep our gaze upon Jesus. We do this by doing what He has commands us to do.

Psalm 119:155 "Salvation is far from the wicked: for they seek not Thy statutes." How true this is. The wicked want nothing to do with God. The faster they can eliminate God from every segment of society; they will finally be rid of the one who judges them (or so they think). You can see that there is a true animosity to the God of heaven. I guess the main reason people hate God is because His way does not satisfy them. They want their fun, and God is in the way. The wicked also have a sense of pride whereby they can figure things out for themselves and they do not need to depend upon anybody (or anything). The very suggestion that they could be wrong on anything is abhorrent to them. Yet, we know that God is superior in every regard. So that is why salvation is far from the wicked. We could also turn the statement around that anyone who does not seek to conform to the statutes of God will be considered wicked. That final category might include some of the nicest, sincerest, even godly people you can imagine. But if they do not follow God's word as He has given to us, they will be lost spiritually (and forever).

Psalm 119:166 "LORD, I have hoped for Thy salvation, and done Thy commandments." We are all longing for salvation. We hope for salvation. One thing we see from past and present is that those who do the commandments of God are the ones who will go to heaven. Matthew 7:21 reads: "Not everyone who says to Me, Lord, Lord, shall enter the kingdom of heaven, but he who does the will of My Father who is in heaven" (NASV). Even Jesus admonished those who claimed to follow Him with these words in Luke 6:46: "Why call me Lord, Lord, and do not the things I say?" (NASV). We must do all the commandments that God has given to us. Why would anyone take a chance with their soul to leave some out of their life?

Psalm 119:174 "I have longed for Thy <u>salvation</u>, O LORD; and Thy law is my delight." You will see that those who really and truly love the Bible and strive to live accordingly also are longing for God's salvation. These two go hand in hand and they cannot be separated. That is the very reason to love God's law and delight in it. Psalm 119: 97 reads: "O how I love Thy law! It is my meditation all the day" (Nasv). Knowing that salvation is reserved for those who do God's will on earth, we should all try our very best to learn and keep His commands.

Psalm 132:16 "I will also clothe her priests with <u>salvation</u>: and her saints shall shout aloud for joy."
This is one of the psalms of ascents. We are not sure who wrote it because it does address trusting in the God of David. God expresses a desire to treat those around Zion with blessings. This place will be God's resting place on earth in a symbolic sense. Of course, we realize that God is everywhere and wherever He chooses to be. Mt. Zion was where the temple was erected, and symbolically, is where people could come to approach God.

Psalm 140:7 "O GOD the Lord, the strength of my <u>salvation</u>, Thou hast covered my head in the day of battle."
This is just another reference to the protection that God provides. This is another case of the word salvation meaning deliverance from mine enemies.

Psalm 144:10 "It is He that giveth <u>salvation</u> unto kings: who delivereth David his servant from the hurtful sword."
God does interact in the affairs of men. God picks and chooses who will be kings and those in places of authority. This is hard for us to understand because throughout human history, because many leaders have typically been harsh and mean. Countless millions have suffered at the hands of unrighteous men and women who have oppressed their own people. We may not understand why God would put these types of people in positions of power. Perhaps if they are bad enough, the people just might try to seek God to become their protector.

Psalm 149:4 "For the LORD taketh pleasure in His people: He will beautify the meek with <u>salvation</u>."
The people the Lord takes pleasure in are those who humble themselves before Him, and seek to please Him by being obedient to His word. When salvation is finally realized, it will be a most beautiful thing to see and obtain.

Many of these uses of the word "salvation" are speaking of that inner peace one has when they have turned all their problems over to God. When they turn to Him for protection and the needs of everyday life, they are comforted. God knows what we need and he will provide it when we put Him first in our lives (Matthew 6:33).

Salvation In The Old Testament Prophecy

This section will deal with the use of the the Hebrew word Yshuwah(3444) which is many times translated salvation. The word for salvation is derived from another word, Yasha (3467), originally, this root was believed to mean "to be open, wide or free" When one has plenty of room in which to move, he feels safe and secure, Yasha means, therefore, to be delivered, saved, to get help; to deliver, give victory, to help; to take vengeance; to preserve. Some versions use "rescue" and "defend cause" and some use "saviour" It is noteworthy that the personal name of our Saviour, Jesus, derives from this root. Also in the N.T., when the crowds cried out to Jesus at His triumphal entry, they used the word Hosanna, which is directly traceable to this verb in the O.T. Yasha and its derivatives appear 353 times in the Hebrew Bible. At first, the word pointed to a physical deliverance from very real enemies or catastrophes. Later, the word: "save" developed a theological meaning. God is concerned about our physical well-being, our emotional status, and the salvation of our souls. God has the ability to save us from anything which would harm us. Salvation is God's love in action. There is none outside of Him. Some verses hint at an everlasting salvation which was coming. Some people, like Simeon and Anna (Luke 2:29,30,38) were waiting for it. (Spiros Zodhaites, Hebrew/Greek Key study Bible pg 1733,34)

Let us watch the transformation of this word in its usage from the deliverance from present distress to the inward peace of mind to the hope of a future deliverance that will be for all time.

Isaiah 12:2 "Behold, God is my salvation; I will trust, and not be afraid: for the LORD JEHOVAH is my strength and my song; He also is become my salvation."
As used in the poetry writings, this is the personal self-satisfaction that one has by doing God's will.

Isaiah 12:3 "Therefore with joy shall ye draw water out of the wells of salvation."
Symbolically, salvation is deep and we can only achieve it by doing something. In this verse, we must draw it out of the well in order to benefit it. As long as it stays down in the well, it offers us nothing at all. We may be extremely thirsty, yet it does not quench our thirst until we draw it unto ourselves. And when we receive it, we will receive it with joy. As you read in the book of Acts of the conversions that took place, notice that joy accompanies those who have drawn the water out of the well. I am referring to baptism. All the cases of conversion involve the baptism, after which the recipients went on their way rejoicing. No one ever rejoiced for salvation until after they received it.

Isaiah 17:10 "Because thou hast forgotten the God of thy salvation, and hast not been mindful of the rock of thy strength, therefore shalt thou plant pleasant plants, and shalt set it with strange slips."
Isaiah tells the people of the Northern kingdom, that the reason for their destruction is

their failure to obey God.

Isaiah 25:9 "And it shall be said in that day, Lo, this is our God; we have waited for Him, and He will save us: this is the LORD; we have waited for Him, we will be glad and rejoice in His <u>salvation</u>."
This is prophecy looking forward to a time in the future. This particular prophecy is describing the church and its lack of limitations as far as citizenship. This particular salvation is used in the sense of personal joy, yet "in that day" they will realize a different kind of salvation.

Isaiah 26:1 "In that day shall this song be sung in the land of Judah; We have a strong city; <u>salvation</u> will God appoint for walls and bulwarks."
Walls and bulwarks are descriptive of a fort or some sort of defense. God will defend us. This defense will be the salvation that God offers in our protection or deliverance. Not until after the church is established do the people realize that this salvation is in the form of eternal life.

Isaiah 33:2 "O LORD, be gracious unto us; we have waited for Thee: be Thou their arm every morning, our <u>salvation</u> also in the time of trouble."
Deliverance from nature and enemies is the thought here, both for the individual and for the nation itself.

Isaiah 33:6 "And wisdom and knowledge shall be the stability of thy times, and strength of <u>salvation</u>: the fear of the LORD is his treasure."
"The fear of the lord is the beginning of knowledge; fools despise wisdom and instruction" (NASV). Read the first few verses of Proverbs and see if this is what it is talking about. When one grounds their selves in the word of the Lord, they have stability in their life and God provides deliverance and men can appreciate the treasure that only God provides.

Isaiah 45:8 "Drop down, ye heavens, from above, and let the skies pour down righteousness: let the earth open, and let them bring forth <u>salvation</u>, and let righteousness spring up together; I the LORD have created it."
God is the source of salvation as He is the source of all things. We learn that when we put our trust in God, we bring the possibility of salvation into our lives.

The next few verses deal with God's promises for future restoration of Israel and all nations. Keep in mind, that the people of the Old Testament never realized salvation as being eternal life. This would take place later as the people learned about eternal salvation in the New Testament age.

Isaiah 45:17 "But Israel shall be saved in the LORD with an everlasting <u>salvation</u>: ye shall not be ashamed nor confounded world without end.
As long as Israel is faithful to God, they will be saved and spared from their enemies. Yet we know that they did not remain faithful, and thus lost their kingdom. For the most part, their understanding of salvation was physical, and to couple the word everlasting

with their physical deliverance meant that the salvation would last as long as the hills remained in place. It would last as long as God would exist. We also know that their nation would only last as long as men kept the covenant God made with them.

Isaiah 46:13 "I bring near My righteousness: it shall not be far off, and My salvation shall not tarry: and I will place salvation in Zion for Israel My glory."
God is near. Everyone must learn that fact. God is not slack concerning His promises (2 Peter 3:9). We also know that from Zion would proceed the new covenant. Zion was the spiritual abode of God in the temple on the mount of Zion within the confines of Jerusalem. This was the abode of God in relationship to His people. From Jerusalem the good news of salvation would proceed forth to the utmost parts of the earth. It happened just as the prophets of God spoke it.

Isaiah 49:6 "And he said, It is a light thing that Thou shouldest be My servant to raise up the tribes of Jacob, and to restore the preserved of Israel: I will also give Thee for a light to the Gentiles, that Thou mayest be My salvation unto the end of the earth."
God is speaking to His Messiah, which is His Son. Here are just some of the instructions which are placed upon Jesus from prophecy. Later the New Testament writers would quote this passage as further proof that this was the Son of God, and that believing in Him, one might have eternal life (John 20:31)

Isaiah 49:8 "Thus saith the LORD, In an acceptable time have I heard thee, and in a day of salvation have I helped thee: and I will preserve thee, and give thee for a covenant of the people, to establish the earth, to cause to inherit the desolate heritages;"
The book of Hebrews is written to show the greatness of Christ and how Christ became a new covenant for God's elect. Paul quoted this passage 2 Corinthians 6:2.

Isaiah 51:5 "My righteousness is near; My salvation is gone forth, and Mine arms shall judge the people; the isles shall wait upon Me, and on Mine arm shall they trust."
God and Jesus and the words of Jesus along with the writings of the Holy Spirit will be our judges in the last day (John 12:48). The arms mentioned are those extensions of God which were used to inform us of His will. You might also think of the song from years ago: "Safe In The Arms Of Jesus". This reminds us that we should trust God and not rely upon princes, rulers, or men (Psalm 118:8-9).

Isaiah 51:6 "Lift up your eyes to the heavens, and look upon the earth beneath: for the heavens shall vanish away like smoke, and the earth shall wax old like a garment, and they that dwell therein shall die in like manner: but My salvation shall be forever, and My righteousness shall not be abolished."
Here is an example of the everlasting life. Though they did not understand it, they began to perceive that there was something better in store for God's people. When we get closer to New Testament times, we will find those who believe in the resurrection. These people were looking for a physical bringing back to life of the faithful upon this earth. They still did not understand the great mystery which was hidden from them. "The heavens vanishing away" reminds us of 2 Peter 3:10: "But the day of the Lord will come like a thief, in which the heavens will pass away with a roar and the elements will be

destroyed with intense heat, and the earth and its works will be burned up". (NASV) The "righteousness of God shall not be abolished" should remind us of another passage from Isaiah: "The grass withers, the flower fades, but the word of our God stands forever". It is God's word that teaches us what His righteousness really is. If we follow God's word in our lives, we will be living righteous lives for Him, and He will reward us.

Isaiah 51:8 "For the moth shall eat them up like a garment, and the worm shall eat them like wool: but My righteousness shall be forever, and My salvation from generation to generation."
Compare this with Acts 2:39: "for the promise is for you and your children, and for all who are far off, as many as the Lord our God shall call to Himself."

Isaiah 52:7 "How beautiful upon the mountains are the feet of him that bringeth good tidings, that publisheth peace; that bringeth good tidings of good, that publisheth salvation; that saith unto Zion, Thy God reigneth! "
Compare this with Rom 10:14-15. The "publisheth" is the making known of this salvation whether it be preached or written. While this was spoken many years before the gospel was pronounced, we can be certain that God still looks upon those who share the gospel message with others as beautiful.

Isaiah 52:10 "The LORD hath made bare His holy arm in the eyes of all the nations; and all the ends of the earth shall see the salvation of our God."
Once again, a deliverance is promised for the people of God, which the world will see and recognize Jehovah as a living active God who cares for His righteous ones.
Compare Daniel 4:28-29 and Daniel 5:34-35, and Daniel 6:26-27.

Isaiah 56:1 "Thus saith the LORD, Keep ye judgment, and do justice: for My salvation is near to come, and My righteousness to be revealed."
Simeon and Anna (Luke 2) were waiting for the salvation of the Lord to come. This salvation would be realized through Jesus.
Notice also that God says that His righteousness was to be revealed, or made known sometime in the future. Once again, the righteousness of God was revealed through Jesus.

Isaiah 59:11 "We roar all like bears, and mourn sore like doves: we look for judgment, but there is none; for salvation, but it is far off from us."
This usage is about deliverance from trials and tribulations. But how can salvation be far off from us? When we fail to bring God into our lives and activities, we keep Him at a distance. Our salvation cannot come to us until we are willing to draw near to God.

Isaiah 59:16 "And he saw that there was no man, and wondered that there was no intercessor: therefore His arm brought salvation unto him; and His righteousness, it sustained him."
This is another prophecy that Jesus would be our intercessor. Jesus would be the one to bring salvation and righteousness. No ordinary man could make this happen.

Isaiah 59:17 "For He put on righteousness as a breastplate, and an helmet of salvation upon His head; and He put on the garments of vengeance for clothing, and was clad with zeal as a cloak."
Describing Jesus, notice that Paul gave us the same type of armour in Ephesians 6 we are to wear on a regular basis to fight against Satan. We are to be like Jesus in all ways possible. This is just another way of being like Jesus, when we put on the whole armour of God.

Isaiah 60:18 "Violence shall no more be heard in thy land, wasting nor destruction within thy borders; but thou shalt call thy walls Salvation, and thy gates Praise."
Once again, we have a future promise that those people will never see, and will not be realized until after the church is established. What such language did was to give those people hope for the future. Such comforting words should have been able to carry them through all their trials. Yet we see from the history of Israel, that the people turned away from God once again.

Isaiah 61:10 "I will greatly rejoice in the LORD, my soul shall be joyful in my God; for He hath clothed me with the garments of salvation, He hath covered me with the robe of righteousness, as a bridegroom decketh himself with ornaments, and as a bride adorneth herself with her jewels."
These are more words and thoughts about the Messiah as spoken through prophecy. The book of Revelation makes several suggestions about us keeping our garments white (pure), and clothed with the brightness of heaven. The picture of the bride as we see in Ephesians 5 is a picture of Christ being the bridegroom presenting His beautiful bride to the Father. The bride is His church.

Isaiah 62:1 "For Zion's sake will I not hold my peace, and for Jerusalem's sake I will not rest, until the righteousness thereof go forth as brightness, and the salvation thereof as a lamp that burneth."
Jerusalem will be the beginning point of this salvation. It was first preached by Peter on the day of Pentecost. Keep in mind that the everlasting kingdom that Daniel prophesied about was at hand and that is what John and Jesus proclaimed.
Still, not until the church is established on the day of Pentecost does anyone realize that salvation can be eternal life in a spiritual kingdom and not anything in this material world.

Isaiah 62:11 "Behold, the LORD hath proclaimed unto the end of the world, Say ye to the daughter of Zion, Behold, thy salvation cometh; behold, His reward is with Him, and His work before him."
Jesus is the "Him" God is speaking of. His work was to do the master's bidding. And He did it very well.

Isaiah 63:5 "And I looked, and there was none to help; and I wondered that there was none to uphold: therefore mine own arm brought salvation unto me; and my fury, it upheld me."
Since God found no man worthy to stand up in place as a representative for the people,

He would need to provide a pure soul. In 1 John 4:9-10 we read: "By this the love of God was manifested in us, that God has sent his only begotten Son into the world so that we might live through Him,. In this is love, not that we loved God, but that he loved us and sent his Son to be the propitiation for our sins. (NASV).

Jeremiah 3:23 "Truly in vain is salvation hoped for from the hills, and from the multitude of mountains: truly in the LORD our God is the salvation of Israel."
Jeremiah tried to teach the people to repent and return to serving the Living God, but they constantly rejected Jehovah. As a result, destruction was coming upon them. These people had turned to idols and were worshipping in the high places in the hills.

Lamentations 3:26 "It is good that a man should both hope and quietly wait for the salvation of the LORD."
The only hope that anyone of the Old Testament knew about salvation is realized in the physical realm. This salvation came by one's circumstances or their own internal feelings. The person who relies upon God to provide this salvation is considered good. There are times when we just need to get away from it all and quietly consider the salvation of God and just long for it. Yet at the same time, we still have a duty to God to do the works He has created us for (Ephesians 2:10).

Jonah 2:9 "But I will sacrifice unto Thee with the voice of thanksgiving; I will pay that that I have vowed. Salvation is of the LORD."
Jonah's salvation is from the belly of the great fish.

Micah 7:7 "Therefore I will look unto the LORD; I will wait for the God of my salvation: my God will hear me."
Micah tells us the right place to focus upon. We all should look to the Lord for guidance and instruction. When we do this, God will hear our prayers.

Habakkuk 3:18 "Yet I will rejoice in the LORD, I will joy in the God of my salvation."
Once again, the inner peace from knowing that one is serving God is the meaning of this salvation.

Zechariah 9:9 "Rejoice greatly, O daughter of Zion; shout, O daughter of Jerusalem: behold, thy King cometh unto thee: He is just, and having salvation; lowly, and riding upon an ass, and upon a colt the foal of an ass."
Is there really any question as to where the salvation of God comes from? Who else but Jesus the Christ.

Salvation In The New Testament

In our continued studies on the translated word "salvation", we now enter the New Testament. Here we will see a further transformation of the word into a realized fact. Some of the New Testament passages are just quotes from Old Testament writings and thus will carry the same meaning from the original writings.

The word for salvation in the Greek language is;
Soteria(4991). Taken from the root word Soze (4982) which means "to save". Soteria means "to save", "deliverance", "preservation", "salvation". Used of material and temporal deliverance in some passages. Used of spiritual and eternal deliverance in some passages. Used of the present experience of God's power to deliver in some passages. Used of the future deliverance at the second coming of Christ in some passages. Used inclusively of all the blessings of God in some passages. And occasionally standing for the Savior Himself in two verses. Used as an ascription of praise to God in one passage. And used to describe what God bestows upon us in one passage. (Spiros Zodhaites, Hebrew/Greek Key study Bible pg 1879)

Luke 1:69 "And hath raised up an horn of <u>salvation</u> for us in the house of his servant David;"
Luke 1:77 "To give knowledge of <u>salvation</u> unto his people by the remission of their sins,"
Both of these passages are included in the prophecy of Zacharias, the father of John the Baptist. Both of these discuss the deliverance that God provides for His people. Similar quotes are found in 1 Samuel 2:1, and Psalm 106:10. As we will find out in our further studies, the knowledge of the Christ, the Son of God is what will bring about this salvation.

Luke 2:30 "For mine eyes have seen thy <u>salvation</u>,"
These are the words of Simeon in the temple. Luke describes this person who waited upon the salvation of the Lord. The prophets had written about a coming salvation which would be greater than what they understood salvation to be. This person along with Anna, had been waiting for the proper signs, and now they have come.

Luke 3:6 "And all flesh shall see the <u>salvation</u> of God."
This word is taken from the Greek word "Soterion" (4992) which describes the hope of eternal life, and also is used metaphorically as a helmet in Ephesians 6. This is also the word that Titus 2:11 uses as "Salvation hath appeared unto all men".
This of course is a quotation from Isa 40:5. Here is a case where those in Isaiah's day did not understand what those in the New Testament day understood. By the time Luke was written, the understanding of eternal life had been known for about twenty years.

Luke 19:9 "And Jesus said unto him, This day is <u>salvation</u> come to this house, forsomuch as he also is a son of Abraham."
Zaccheus was a sinner who had just repented to Jesus. Jesus proclaimed that this person would now once again benefit from the blessings that God gives to His faithful ones.

John 4:22 "Ye worship ye know not what: we know what we worship: for <u>salvation</u> is of the Jews."
As Jesus is speaking to the woman at the well, He describes the source of salvation. It is through the promise of blessings given to Abraham and his descendants by God. Also, we can understand that the God of the Jews is the only God that can produce salvation.

Acts 4:12 "Neither is there <u>salvation</u> in any other: for there is none other name under heaven given among men, whereby we must be saved."
Here is the first recorded instance of salvation being used as something eternal in nature. Pretty much throughout the rest of the New Testament "salvation" will carry a meaning of eternal consequences. Notice also now, that we are now in the "last days" or the "Christian dispensation". This salvation is that which saves us from our current problems, as well as provides a future deliverance in the end times.

Acts 13:26 "Men and brethren, children of the stock of Abraham, and whosoever among you feareth God, to you is the word of this <u>salvation</u> sent."
Paul gives a very brief history of the Jewish people and proclaims that the salvation promised by God via the prophets is that which Paul and his companions are proclaiming.

Acts 13:47 "For so hath the Lord commanded us, saying, I have set thee to be a light of the Gentiles, that thou shouldest be for <u>salvation</u> unto the ends of the earth."
Here, Paul is quoting Isaiah 42:6 as he describes to the Jews that their rejection is what caused the Gospel to be taken to the Gentiles who would receive it with gladness.

Acts 16:17 "The same followed Paul and us, and cried, saying, These men are the servants of the most high God, which show unto us the way of <u>salvation</u>."
Of course, Paul was a little put out because of the girl with the spirit of divination, but she was speaking the truth. Paul and his companions were bringing the teaching of a way of salvation which had not been realized before that time for those people.

Acts 28:28 "Be it known therefore unto you, that the <u>salvation</u> of God is sent unto the Gentiles, and that they will hear it."
Paul had just quoted Isaiah 6:9-10. Once again, Paul tells the Jews that they have rejected the salvation of God, but that the Gentiles eagerly wait for it and will receive it.

Romans 1:16 "For I am not ashamed of the gospel of Christ: for it is the power of God unto <u>salvation</u> to everyone that believeth; to the Jew first, and also to the Greek."
This usage is in the sense of deliverance from the bondage of sin, and also the

promised hope of a relationship with God, realized in an eternal existence. Notice, that there are conditions placed upon receiving this salvation. We will examine this in the last chapter.

Romans 10:10 "For with the heart man believeth unto righteousness; and with the mouth confession is made unto <u>salvation</u>."
This usage is the deliverance of the spiritual and eternal nature. Although confession is necessary, it cannot be implied that confession is all that is needed to obtain this salvation. One still has to meet all the requirements that God has given in order to be saved.

Romans 11:11 "I say then, Have they stumbled that they should fall? God forbid: but rather through their fall <u>salvation</u> is come unto the Gentiles, for to provoke them to jealousy."
Paul had just quoted Isaiah 29:10 and Psalms 69:22-23.
The message is that some of God's chosen would reject the way of salvation provided through Jesus Christ. And as a result, the message would be taken to the Gentiles to satisfy the needs of all mankind. Naturally this would upset the Jews because they thought they were the only ones entitled to be recipients of the grace of God.

Romans 13:11 "And that, knowing the time, that now it is high time to awake out of sleep: for now is our <u>salvation</u> nearer than when we believed."
This usage of the word is discussing the eternal home in Heaven with God. Once we have obeyed the gospel and been saved from our past sins, we must labor on seeking the great reward of the faithful. The longer we live serving the Lord, the closer this salvation can be realized.

2 Corinthians 1:6 "And whether we be afflicted, it is for your consolation and <u>salvation,</u> which is effectual in the enduring of the same sufferings which we also suffer: or whether we be comforted, it is for your consolation and <u>salvation</u>."
Paul is using this as a present deliverance from sin and oppression. Paul's example should serve as a model for those people to follow. We also should follow the model of Paul.

2 Corinthians 6:2 "(For he saith, I have heard thee in a time accepted, and in the day of <u>salvation</u> have I succoured thee: behold, now is the accepted time; behold, now is the day of salvation.)"
Paul takes a quotation from Isaiah 49:8 and makes an application for all people. Why put off your salvation. Today is the best time to be saved. Do not take a chance that something could prevent you from accepting Christ as your source of eternal salvation. Just do it now.

2 Corinthians 7:10 "For godly sorrow worketh repentance to <u>salvation</u> not to be repented of: but the sorrow of the world worketh death."
Salvation can be obtained, but it requires certain actions and deeds to be reached. For in the case of a fallen child of God, they must work repentance because of the sorrow

they have. Working repentance is an action that shows we really have changed our hearts and course of action.

Ephesians 1:13 "In whom ye also trusted, after that ye heard the word of truth, the gospel of your salvation: in whom also after that ye believed, ye were sealed with that Holy Spirit of promise,"
Here, the word is used in the sense of a present deliverance mixed in with the future hope. Notice it is the gospel of Christ that gives us this hope. The gospel of Christ is the source of our salvation.

Ephesians 6:17 "And take the helmet of salvation, and the sword of the Spirit, which is the word of God."
Used metaphorically to describe a sort of protection, we must learn that the hope of our salvation should keep us in constant duty to God.

Philippians 1:19 "For I know that this shall turn to my salvation through your prayer, and the supply of the Spirit of Jesus Christ,"
Paul is describing a deliverance from prison. The NASV uses the word "deliverance" instead of salvation.

Philippians 1:28 "And in nothing terrified by your adversaries: which is to them an evident token of perdition, but to you of salvation, and that of God."
If the Philippians conduct themselves in a manner worthy of the Gospel (v.27) and stand firm in it, their adversaries will see the sign of destruction, but the faithful will realize salvation.

Philippians 2:12 "Wherefore, my beloved, as ye have always obeyed, not as in my presence only, but now much more in my absence, work out your own salvation with fear and trembling."
Used in both senses of present deliverance from the bondage of sin, and the hope of eternal life. We also get the sense that we have a part in our salvation. It takes work on our part to realize it.

1 Thessalonians 5:8 "But let us, who are of the day, be sober, putting on the breastplate of faith and love; and for an helmet, the hope of salvation."
This passage more closely looks at the metaphor of the helmet and is more meaningful than Ephesians 6:17. It is because this passage describes it as the hope of salvation.

1 Thessalonians 5:9 "For God hath not appointed us to wrath, but to obtain salvation by our Lord Jesus Christ,"
Through Jesus Christ we can be saved spiritually and eternally.

2 Thessalonians 2:13 "But we are bound to give thanks alway to God for you, brethren beloved of the Lord, because God hath from the beginning chosen you
to salvation through sanctification of the Spirit and belief of the truth."
Notice that God made provisions that whoever would meet certain qualifications would

receive salvation. Those who would reject those conditions would not receive salvation. The idea of predestination might be considered here. What many believe about predestination is wrong. God tells us what kind of person can be saved. God does not choose each individual and assign them their destination. Everyone does that on their own.

2 Timothy 2:10 "Therefore I endure all things for the elect's sakes, that they may also obtain the salvation which is in Christ Jesus with eternal glory."
This usage is the eternal life salvation.

2 Timothy 3:15 "And that from a child thou hast known the holy scriptures, which are able to make thee wise unto salvation through faith which is in Christ Jesus."
The scriptures are the Old Testament. They would serve as a guide and tutor. They declared the future promise of salvation through Christ Jesus the Messiah.

Titus 2:11 "For the grace of God that bringeth salvation hath appeared to all men."
Salvation can only come from God. God's grace brought it to man. The gospel is that which saves. The gospel is the grace of God. That which we need for salvation is the grace of God. Many times, the grace of God and the gospel are the same thing.

Hebrews 1:14 "Are they not all ministering spirits, sent forth to minister for them who shall be heirs of salvation?"
Speaking of angels, the writer is telling us that God is taking care of His children.

Hebrews 2:3 "How shall we escape, if we neglect so great salvation; which at the first began to be spoken by the Lord, and was confirmed unto us by them that heard Him."
The usage is deliverance and future hope. This also serves as a reminder that salvation is acquired by our choice. Some will teach that you cannot neglect the salvation of God on your own. But this verse confirms that one can neglect the salvation that God offers.

Hebrews 2:10 "For it became him, for whom are all things, and by whom are all things, in bringing many sons unto glory, to make the captain of their salvation perfect through sufferings."
This one described as our captain is Jesus Christ. Further studies in the book of Hebrews will bear this out.

Hebrews 5:9 "And being made perfect, he became the author of eternal salvation unto all them that obey him;"
Through His sufferings, Jesus endured the cross, and as a result, if we follow Him, we shall be saved eternally.

Hebrews 9:28 "So Christ was once offered to bear the sins of many; and unto them that look for Him shall He appear the second time without sin unto salvation."
Eternal life is promised for the continued faithful. The sacrifice of Christ was sufficient to provide salvation for all time and for every person who would come to Him in faith.

1 Peter 1:5 "Who are kept by the power of God through faith unto <u>salvation</u> ready to be revealed in the last time."
Hope and deliverance is how this is used.

1 Peter 1:9-10 "Receiving the end of your faith, even the <u>salvation</u> of your souls. Of which <u>salvation</u> the prophets have inquired and searched diligently, who prophesied of the grace that should come unto you."
This is the eternal life salvation which will be the end result of our faithfulness to all of God's will. Notice that the prophets wanted to know, but it was revealed to them that they could not have it. See Daniel 12. It was not for them, but it was for those of the Christian dispensation.

2 Peter 3:15 "And account that the longsuffering of our Lord is <u>salvation</u>; even as our beloved brother Paul also according to the wisdom given unto him hath written unto you."
God is patient with us more than we deserve. As a result, God gives us more opportunities to put our lives on the right track. We should all thank Him for that.

Jude 1:3 "Beloved, when I gave all diligence to write unto you of the common <u>salvation</u>, it was needful for me to write unto you, and exhort you that ye should earnestly contend for the faith which was once delivered unto the saints."
All saints share in this common salvation. The saints of the New Testament are those who are obedient servants of God also known as "Christians".

Revelation 7:10 "And cried with a loud voice, saying, <u>Salvation</u> to our God which sitteth upon the throne, and unto the Lamb."
Here the word is used in such a way as to describe what God has done for us. Since God provided salvation for us, we in turn by our acceptance and obedience provide a form of reciprocal effect. In other words, we offer to God the blessings that he bestows upon us.

Revelation 12:10 "And I heard a loud voice saying in heaven, Now is come <u>salvation</u>, and strength, and the kingdom of our God, and the power of his Christ: for the accuser of our brethren is cast down, which accused them before our God day and night."
This verse is possibly describing the second coming of Christ. As Christ comes to deal out retribution to those who know not God, and keep not His commandments (2 Thessalonians 1:8), it is inferred that salvation is coming to those who keep His commandments and truly know Him.

Revelation 19:1 "And after these things I heard a great voice of much people in heaven, saying, Alleluia; <u>Salvation</u>, and glory, and honour, and power, unto the Lord our God:"
In ultimate praise to Almighty God, we offer our blessings for what God has provided for us. God has made the provision of eternal salvation, and now it is up to us how we will handle that provision.

A Study Of The Word "Eternal"

This section will deal with the word "eternal". This comes from the Hebrew word "Owlam(5769)". This Hebrew noun comes from 5956. It is what is hidden, concealed (i.e., to the vanishing point); time immemorial, time past, antiquity (from the most ancient times, Gen 6:4; 1 Sam 27:8; Isa 63:16; Jer 2:20; 5:15; Ps 25:6); eternity, the distant future (terminus ad quem); duration, perpetual, without end, always, everlasting time; lifetime. In the plural form it means ages or endless times. The KJV translates the word as "beginning of the world" in Isa 64:4 and as "world" in Ps 73:12 and Ecc 3:11. There are 440 occurrences of Owlam in the Hebrew Old Testament. More than 300 of these instances indicate an indefinite continuance into the very near future. however the meaning of the word is not confined to the future. There are at least twenty instances where Owlam clearly refers to the past, though rately a limitless past. Deut 32:7 and Job 22:15 point to the time of one's elders. Prov 22:28; 23:10; Jer 6:16; 18:15; 28:8 seem to go back even further. Sometimes the time just pr ior to the exile is referred to (Isa 58:12; 61:4, Mic 7:14; Mal 3:4; Ezra 4:15,19). At other times it goes back further, to the events of the exodus from Egypt (1 Sam 27:8; Isa 51:9; 63:9,11). Gen 6:4 indicates the time shortly before the flood. The basic meaning of Owlam is "most distant times," whether the remote past or the future, depending upon the accompanying prepositions. Therefore, Owlam is a broad range between the remotest time and perpetuity (from the viewpoint of the speaker). Here are some examples; eternity in the sense of not being limited to the present (Ecc 3:11); remotest time (1 Chron 16:36), either at the very beginning (Isa 46:9) or from pre-creation until now (Psa 25:6); from older times (Gen 6:4), for a long time (Isa 42:14); long ago (Jer 2:20); formerly, in ancient times (Josh 24:2); never (when used with the negative, Isa 63:19); into the indefinite future (Deut 23:3); forever (i.e. from the time of the speaker forward, 1 Sam 1:22); as long as one lives (i.e. a simple duration extended into the indefinite future, Ex 21:6); continuity without change (Gen 3:22); day by day (Psa 61:7,8); the most distant future (Gen 9:16); without beginning, without end and ever-continuing (Isa 26:4). Owlam, the same Hebrew word, can describe a short period of only three days (though it must have seemed like an eternity to Jonah as "forever", Jon 2:6) or it can be used in conjunction with God--the God of eternity, the everlasting God, God forever. Temporal categories are inadequate to describe the nature of God's existence. The Creator has been "from everlasting to everlasting" (Psa 90:2). Even then, it still express the idea of a continued, measurable existence, rather than a state of being independent of time considerations. El Owlam, "The Everlasting God", was predominantly associated with Beersheba (Gen 21:33). The God of Abraham was not touched by the vicissitudes of time. Compare Isa 40:28 'Ad (5703) which has about the same spectrum of meaning as owlam. the Septuagint generally translates owlam by aion(G165)cf. New Testament Lexical section, referring to a long age or period of time, often translated as "world".
(Spiros Zodhaites, Hebrew/Greek Key Study Bible pg. 1757)

Deuteronomy 33:27 "The eternal God is thy refuge, and underneath are the everlasting arms: and He shall thrust out the enemy from before thee; and shall say, Destroy them.

Of course, everyone knew that God was forever. God had been from everlasting and will last forever."
The earth was also considered as being eternal, because it had been there throughout their generations. The only thing that was not eternal was their existence. They knew that all men die (Hebrews 9:27). The hills, valleys, and streams were there before they were born, and they realize they will be there long after they are dead. In Old Testament times, the people did not realize that their souls would continue forever. That fact would remain a mystery until the gospel was to be preached in the New Testament.

Isaiah 60:15 "Whereas thou hast been forsaken and hated, so that no man went through thee, I will make thee an eternal excellency, a joy of many generations."
This passage is in a chapter that speaks of the hope of future Israel by the prophet. God expressed that in the future, things would be better and His people will be blessed. So anything done for God, it was hoped, would be remembered by God for as long as He existed (which was forever).

Daniel 12:2 "And many of those who sleep in the dust of the ground will awake, these to everlasting life, but the others to disgrace and everlasting contempt."(NASV)
We see that the word translated "everlasting" is the same word that is often translated eternal (the Hebrew word "owlam"). This word implies an existence beyond what the human experience is used to. If you notice in this passage context, the words of eternal life caught the attention of Daniel. He was not familiar with such a meaning that life would continue. Of course, Daniel was thinking physically. Daniel even made inquiry about this salvation and was told to seal up what he had written. Peter wrote about the prophecies long ago where the prophets made inquiry as to this salvation (1 Peter 1:10-12). You will notice in the beginning of the New Testament that there were many inquiries about this eternal life Jesus had begun to preach about. Most of them were thinking physically, whereas Jesus was speaking spiritually.

Now, in the New Testament the word begins to evolve into something else. It is used to indicate not only a present future, but a continued existence after life is over. Notice, as you read these passages, the association with the surrounding words. Not only is God eternal, but life, death, punishment, salvation, and other things become eternal as well. Once the gospel is preached, people will begin to realize that they have an immortal soul which will not perish because of death. As they realize the eternal nature of a soul, they need an incentive to be diligent in pursuit of heaven. When people forget about their soul, they lose interest of the things of God.

The Greek word often translated eternal is Aionios(166); eternal, belonging to the aion(165), to time in its duration, constant, abiding, eternal. When referring to eternal life, the life which is Gods and hence not affected by the limitations of time,. Aionios is specifically predicated of the saving blessings of divine revelation, denoting not belonging to wht is transitory. Meanings: (1) Having neither beginning nor end (Rom,.16:26; Heb. 9:14). (2) Without end (Mt 25:41,46; 2 Thess 1:9, etc,). In Philem 15, forever, not only during the term of one's natural life, but through endless ages of eternal life and blessedness. (3) In Jude 7, eternal fire refers to the miraculous fire from heaven which destroyed the cities of Sodom and Gommorha, not only because the effect thereof shall be of equal duration with the world, but also because the burning of those cities is a dreadful emblem of that everlasting fire (Mt 25:41) which awaits the ungodly and unclean (cf 2 Pet) 2:6. (4)Chronoi, times, aionioi, eternal means the ages of the world, the times seince the beginning of its existence (Rom 16:25; 2 Tim 1:9; Tit 1:2; cf Eph 1:4; 1 Pet 1:20) (Spiros Zodhaites, Hebrew/Greek Key Study Bible pg. 1801)

We will notice in the gospel accounts several who request information on how to obtain eternal life. We must keep in mind that their concept of eternal life was limited to the physical realm at that time. They did not yet comprehend that Jesus was speaking in spiritual terms. Let us now, notice the gospel passages that use the word "eternal".

Matthew 19:16 ""And, behold, one came and said unto him, Good Master, what good thing shall I do, that I may have <u>eternal life</u>?
What was the intention and motivation of the person known as the rich young ruler? It was the prospect of living forever. Remember that their understanding was limited at this time. They were young and alive and really just like our youth today. They take very little consideration of the end of their lives. They behave as if they will live forever. Remember that when Jesus began His ministry, He was talking about the kingdom of heaven and how great it would be. Well, people were ready for the kingdom now; they did not want to wait, neither did they understand it was limited to the spiritual realm.

Matthew 25:46 "And these shall go away into everlasting punishment: but the righteous into <u>life eternal.</u>"
The great judgment scene found here and in Revelation 20 are the only glimpses of what that day will be like. There will be a great gathering of all accountable souls who have ever lived. They will be judged by the things they did. A judgment for all mankind was recognized throughout the Bible. The prophet Jeremiah has many references to the fact that God will bring them to judgment. Notice here that there are only two possible pronouncements of judgment. We call them heaven or hell, and this is the destiny of all men. Hebrews 9:27 tells us: "And inasmuch as it is appointed for man to die once and after this comes judgment." (NASV)

Mark 3:29 "But he that shall blaspheme against the Holy Ghost hath never forgiveness, but is in danger of <u>eternal damnation</u>."
While our goal is to express the duration of damnation, we must also realize this was spoken in the context of the Old Law being in force. Blasphemy against God was considered one of the worst of all crimes any person could commit. For those of that day, speaking anything against God was blasphemy. But when Jesus told the paralytic that his sins were forgiven, the crowd charged Jesus with blasphemy because they considered only God had such power to remove sins. It was quite obvious that blasphemy would bring damnation to anyone under the old Law, and such could not ever be forgiven. We really need to be thankful that we live under a system of grace that even if someone spoke blasphemy that by a sincere heart they could be forgiven of such trespass. We will deal with this in a later chapter.

Mark 10:17 "And when he was gone forth into the way, there came one running, and kneeled to him, and asked him, Good Master, what shall I do that I may inherit eternal life?"
This is the same context from Matthew 19:16.

Mark 10:30 "But he shall receive an hundredfold now in this time, houses, and brethren, and sisters, and mothers, and children, and lands, with persecutions; and in the world to come eternal life.
After the question from verse 26 "then who can be saved? (NASV), Jesus responded that with God it was possible. Men would find it impossible for anyone to be saved. As long as men and women were focused upon satisfying their physical needs, they would fall short. But those who would seek the Lord and focus upon their spiritual needs would find an abundance of the blessings that were hidden there in plain sight. When we live our life for Jesus, we receive one hundred fold the blessings that we may give up of this world. The greatest blessing is ultimately, eternal life in heaven.

Luke 10:25 "And, behold, a certain lawyer stood up, and tempted him, saying, Master, what shall I do to inherit eternal life?
One concept of how to receive eternal life is to think that we can earn or merit it by doing good works. While we will spend a lot of time speaking of how good works will help us get to heaven, we must also add that by themselves, good works mean nothing for our salvation. Salvation comes from God, and only God can offer salvation. So in one sense, good works do not save us, but we also will see that we cannot be saved without good works. Is this a contradiction? It's more like a paradox. We will see that viewing our salvation as something earned is just as wrong as it can be because it is God who offers His grace to us that brings our salvation. Some people seem to grasp onto this concept and teach a doctrine that teaches man does not need to do anything to acquire the grace of God. But in order to teach such a doctrine, they have to ignore practically all the rest of scripture to teach such.

John 3:15 "That whosoever believeth in him should not perish, but have eternal life."
The offer of eternal life comes from Jesus. The reading of the NASV is more enlightening: "that whoever believes may in Him have eternal life." This places the emphasis of salvation upon God and removes it from man. Man can do nothing on his own to merit eternal salvation, and we will find that salvation is the gift of God. But then we have to immediately turn around and emphasize that our actions are totally responsible of whether we are saved or lost eternally. This is a paradox.

John 3:16 "For God so loved the world, that he gave His only begotten Son, that whoever believes in him should not perish, but have eternal life."
This by far is one of the most well-known passages of scripture. For in it, many find that the "faith only" doctrine is supported. And if there were no other scripture to teach us our duty to God, it is plausible that "faith only" would bring salvation. Many hold to this passage and teach that belief in Jesus is all you need to bring salvation to yourself. What they do is ignore other passages that even Jesus spoke which places accountability upon all men. Rarely in the context of John 3:16 discussions will you

hear what Jesus says down in verse 36: "He who believes in the Son has eternal life; but he who does not obey the Son shall not see life, but the wrath of God abides on him." (NASV)

John 4:36 "And he that reapeth receiveth wages, and gathereth fruit unto life eternal: that both he that soweth and he that reapeth may rejoice together."
The disciples had gone into town to buy food, and Jesus stayed behind where He encountered the woman at the well. Jesus spoke to her about water where one who partook would never thirst again, and He had food that the partaker would never be hungry again. This was on the mind of Jesus when the disciples returned and begged Him to eat. He spoke of His spiritual food as being the work of preaching that He was doing. His whole life was dedicated to pleasing God. He spoke of harvesting the fields, and we know from the context, Jesus was speaking of evangelizing souls being a group effort. It does not matter who planted, watered, or reaped. Everyone who participates will enjoy the bounty. And the bounty is described as eternal life.

John 5:39 "Search the scriptures; for in them ye think ye have eternal life: and they are they which testify of me."
God revealed through Moses and the prophets that the Messiah would come to deliver the people. The people always were looking for a man to come along and conquer the world, and make all people subject to them. This is especially true of the Pharisees. So Jesus came and was speaking in spiritual terms, and they were looking for physical things, and Jesus did not bring them what they wanted to hear, they became angry and wanted to find a way to get rid of Jesus. They were eventually successful and they brought us the greatest thing from human history. They brought about the death on the cross by the Son of God. The Pharisees did us a big favor by killing Jesus. They actually brought us eternal life, which was God's plan from the beginning.

John 6:54 "Whoso eateth my flesh, and drinketh my blood, hath eternal life; and I will raise him up at the last day."
Some want to take this literally which would be cannibalism. Yet we learn quickly that what Jesus was speaking about was the work that He came to do. We are to partake in His work. What is this work? Helping souls get to heaven is the work in the grand scheme of things. That is why God sent the Son. That is why Jesus came. That is why the Holy Spirit brought us the Bible. That is why every child of God needs to evangelize.

John 6:68 "Then Simon Peter answered him, Lord, to whom shall we go? thou hast the words of eternal life."
Peter recognized that if Jesus is the Son of God, His words actually came from God. The words of Jesus can bring us eternal life. But eternal life is only available to us if we follow His commands. Just because words were written about salvation does not mean that salvation is a given. These words tell us how to obtain salvation. We have to comply with the instructions given to us in His word, the Bible. And yes, these words can produce salvation for those who hear and believe and obey.

John 10:28 "And I give unto them eternal life; and they shall never perish, neither shall

any man pluck them out of my hand."
Here is another passage that many in the world misuse. They teach that one can never fall from God's protective hand. While it is true that no force of any kind, either physical or spiritual, can pull us away from God; there is ample evidence that a person may choose to leave the protective care of God and fall away and lose their salvation.

John 12:25 "He that loveth his life shall lose it; and he that hateth his life in this world shall keep it unto life eternal. "

John 17:2 "As thou hast given him power over all flesh, that he should give eternal life to as many as thou hast given him. "

John 17:3 "And this is life eternal, that they might know thee the only true God, and Jesus Christ, whom thou hast sent."
As you read the three passages above, you will notice a sort of transformation from a physical existence into a spiritual existence. Though eternal life was taught, it was not fully comprehended. This was a part of the great mystery. This is part of the mystery that will be made known through the Church (Ephesians 3:10).
Now as we get into the gospel age, we will notice that the word takes upon itself a completely spiritual meaning.

Acts 13:48 "And when the Gentiles heard this, they were glad, and glorified the word of the Lord: and as many as were ordained to eternal life believed."
Though it is the same language used by our Lord, the hearers had concepts within their mind on what this really meant. Now that the church has come into existence, and is built upon the foundation of Christ and the apostle's doctrine, we will see more and more that an understanding of forever existence is realized. We should also have a discussion about the word "ordained" as used in this passage. We usually see the word in a context of some religious ritual. What it means here is that God has already ordained (or established) what requirements would be needed to obtain eternal salvation. Those who meet the requirements are those who have fulfilled their duty to God, and thus have been ordained. Do not read anything more than that which is recorded in scripture.

Romans 1:20 "For the invisible things of him from the creation of the world are clearly seen, being understood by the things that are made, even his eternal power and Godhead; so that they are without excuse."
Here the power of God is being spoken of. This power has no expiration date and will continue forever.

Romans 2:7 "To them who by patient continuance in well doing seek for glory and honour and immortality, eternal life.'
Here, we see that eternal life is equated with immortality. This is the first time that this concept is seen in the scripture. It has been hinted at, and there have been many suggestions made as to what the possibility of our existence could be. Here we have it in written form that eternal life is associated with our soul and continual existence.

Romans 5:21 "That as sin hath reigned unto death, even so might grace reign through righteousness unto eternal life by Jesus Christ our Lord."
This teaches that there are certain requirements to receive this eternal life. Of course all souls will continue eternally. Most of the time in New Testament scripture, we see that eternal life is found in relation to the faithful of God who will be allowed entrance into heaven. Usually eternal death, separation, or punishment are reserved for those who are unfaithful to God. This passage teaches that through righteousness (continued), one can have the reward of heaven.

Romans 6:23 "For the wages of sin is death; but the gift of God is eternal life through Jesus Christ our Lord."
We cannot have eternal life without Jesus Christ. Jesus taught that He was the door, and that nobody could approach the Father except through Him. Notice also how this is associated with the grace of God. And it is offered to us as in the form of a gift (John 3:16).

2 Corinthians 4:17 "For our light affliction, which is but for a moment, worketh for us a far more exceeding and eternal weight of glory."
I love this passage. No matter what Satan and the world has thrown our way to keep us out of heaven and the trials it puts us through; all the heartache and pain we suffer is described as nothing compared to what God has provided for us. The glory that belongs to Jesus now, will be available to us when we get to heaven. No matter how great, wonderful, or awesome you can imagine heaven to be, we have the assurance from God that it will be far better than we can even imagine. Why take a chance on losing your soul for a moment's pleasure?

2 Corinthians 4:18 "While we look not at the things which are seen, but at the things which are not seen: for the things which are seen are temporal; but the things which are not seen are eternal."
Of course, Paul is talking about God and salvation. He surely is not talking about peoples, sights, and events in other parts of the world. Things of the spiritual realm are eternal. Not only God is eternal, but our souls are as well. The only difference is that we had a beginning, whereas God has always been.

2 Corinthians 5:1 "For we know that if our earthly house of this tabernacle were dissolved, we have a building of God, an house not made with hands, eternal in the heavens."
Paul is discussing the everlasting soul within each person and the place where that eternal soul will dwell. For the righteous of the earth, heaven is the final destination while the wicked will be sent to everlasting torment. This building is much greater than our earthly tent we dwell in (our human body). It will be the place where all God's righteous ones will dwell (heaven). There in heaven we will have peace for nobody will consider self above anything else. There will be no sin, selfishness, pride, greed, division, or problems in heaven. God will be the focus of our existence forevermore.

Ephesians 3:11 "According to the eternal purpose which he purposed in Christ Jesus our Lord."
Paul just described the mystery of God and how it no longer is a mystery, because these hidden things were revealed through the church. Take time to read Ephesians 3:1-11. Also we notice, that God had this purpose (plan) before time began. This purpose was designed before the foundation of the world and before He said "let there be light". God has always had a plan for the redemption of mankind.

1 Timothy 1:17 "Now unto the King eternal, immortal, invisible, the only wise God, be honour and glory for ever and ever. Amen."
Several descriptions of God are presented here.

1 Timothy 6:12 "Fight the good fight of faith, lay hold on eternal life, whereunto thou art also called, and hast professed a good profession before many witnesses."
Eternal life is within our grasp. We can acquire it. It takes a lifetime to accomplish. It is not easy, but it is simple. Each individual is responsible for their own salvation and where they will end up in eternity.

1 Timothy 6:19 "Laying up in store for themselves a good foundation against the time to come, that they may lay hold on eternal life."
Used in the same sense as in the previous verse. Paul was giving instruction to Timothy to tell the rich that they had the opportunity and means to do for others. It was actually a responsibility for those with the means to assist those in need. If these rich people would seek to provide for the better welfare of the needy, it would prove their hearts were in the right place, and God would reward them with eternal life in heaven.

2 Timothy 2:10 "Therefore I endure all things for the elect's sakes, that they may also obtain the salvation which is in Christ Jesus with eternal glory.
Our glory will be the salvation that can only come through Christ. Paul also is teaching that it is not a granted thing, but an earned thing, this salvation. Paul is speaking of his personal responsibility and doing God's commands that will bring about his salvation.

Titus 1:2 "In hope of eternal life, which God, that cannot lie, promised before the world began."
Yes, God had it all arranged before He even said "Let there be light". Notice also that it is the hope of eternal life that we are seeking to obtain. God promised this and it is realized through our faith and obedience to Jesus Christ which is the working of God's grace.

Titus 3:7 "That being justified by his grace, we should be made heirs according to the hope of eternal life."
Part of our study on "salvation" shows that "hope" is a major part in the concept of salvation. Look especially to the prophets and New Testament use of "salvation". It is something they wanted to know about, and in the New Testament, it was something that was possible to obtain.

Hebrews 5:9 "And being made perfect, he became the author of eternal salvation unto all them that obey him."
Here the words are associated together as a single entity. Although as we study, we find the word salvation has an eternal quality. Eternal life is the ultimate salvation.

Hebrews 6:2 "Of the doctrine of baptisms, and of laying on of hands, and of resurrection of the dead, and of eternal judgment. "
This eternal judgment does not mean judgment will last forever, it is speaking of the result of our judgment. Once we die, our judgment is sealed. And whatever judgement we receive, it will be forever. There is nothing anyone or anything can do to change one's status after death. That is why it is so important in this life to be right with God and to be prepared for death.

Hebrews 9:12 "Neither by the blood of goats and calves, but by his own blood he entered in once into the holy place, having obtained eternal redemption for us."
God's redemption through His Son, will last forever providing we remain faithful in this life.

Hebrews 9:14 "How much more shall the blood of Christ, who through the eternal Spirit offered himself without spot to God, purge your conscience from dead works to serve the living God?"
Christ is just as eternal as God and the Holy Spirit, because the Three are One in spirit, character, unity, purpose, and love.

Hebrews 9:15 "And for this cause he is the mediator of the new testament, that by means of death, for the redemption of the transgressions that were under the first testament, they which are called might receive the promise of eternal inheritance."
An inheritance is given to heirs. Romans 8:16-17 explains how that we are heirs of God and fellow heirs with Christ. What belongs to Christ now (the glory and favor of God) will be ours when we overcome all the obstacles of life and reach heaven (Colossians 3:3-4).

1 Peter 5:10 "But the God of all grace, who hath called us unto his eternal glory by Christ Jesus, after that ye have suffered a while, make you perfect, stablish, strengthen, settle you."
This is speaking of the relationship we have with God, Christ, and the Holy Spirit. If we will be faithful to God and follow His commandments, we will share in the glory of God. 1 John 3:2 says that we will be like Him, and Colossians 3:4 tells us that we will share in His glory that He now possesses. Once we get to heaven, Christ will abandon the glory He currently has and assume His rightful position at the center of heaven.

1 John 1:2 "(For the life was manifested, and we have seen it, and bear witness, and show unto you that eternal life, which was with the Father, and was manifested unto us)."
What was manifested was the incarnation of Jesus. Jesus was the Messiah, the chosen and anointed of God. Jesus the man was God in the flesh. John is writing to

help people understand that Jesus was God and that Jesus was the way to God and eternal life.

1 John 2:25 "And this is the promise that he hath promised us, even eternal life." Eternal life is promised to the faithful of God. It is not promised to everyone. It is offered to all men (Titus 2:11), but only those who accept it and agree to live by its terms will be able to enter heaven and live there eternally.

1 John 3:15 "Whosoever hateth his brother is a murderer: and ye know that no murderer hath eternal life abiding in him."
This passage teaches that we may be in posession of eternal life in this life, yet unless we remain faithful, we can lose that eternal life. It is like paying an airfare and holding our boarding pass to get on the plane. Just because we have a boarding pass does not mean we will get to our destination. We still have to abide by the rules, or we can be taken away by the authorities. Yes, we have the promise of eternal life, but we will not realize it unless we have been faithful, and God invites us into heaven on judgment day.

1 John 5:11 "And this is the record, that God hath given to us eternal life, and this life is in his Son."
The scriptures emphasize that life eternal is only through Jesus Christ.

1 John 5:13 "These things have I written unto you that believe on the name of the Son of God; that ye may know that ye have eternal life, and that ye may believe on the name of the Son of God."
If we are faithful, we can have that confidence that God will be pleased with us and invite us in. We also know that this will only happen if we are faithful until death. Thank God for His mercy and provisions that we can have this wonderful hope.

Jude 1:7 "Even as Sodom and Gomorrha, and the cities about them in like manner, giving themselves over to fornication, and going after strange flesh, are set forth for an example, suffering the vengeance of eternal fire."
As we have concentrated on eternal life, the scripture also associates the fires of hell as being eternal. Since the torment will be eternal, we must not cease from warning those on the wrong path to change their course of action for their lives and come into a relationship with Him. They must confess Jesus as Lord, and submit to His will by obedience to His commands.

Since the word "owlam" appears over four hundred times in the Old Testament, we have only used a few examples. The same goes for the Greek word "Aionios" in the New Testament. These examples should be more than sufficient to help us understand the words and their meanings as used in Scripture.

The Three Salvations Of The New Testament

In the New Testament, we see three different kinds of salvation. Correctly stated, we see three aspects of salvation. We must be careful to recognize the three distinct salvations and keep them in their context so as to not cause confusion. Each of these three salvations is distinct and each one has its own outcome.

The first salvation that Jesus and the apostles address is the salvation from our sins. While we have sin associated with our life, we do not have God in our life (Ephesians 2:1-3). Paul explains that before we become a Christian we are separated from God and we have no hope of eternal life. When we obey the gospel teaching and are baptized for the remission of sins, we have our sins washed away (Acts 22:16) and removed from our record. As long as we had sin in our life, we were separated from God (Isaiah 59:2). We could say in a sense that God did not want anything to do with us (1 John 1:5) because we were stained with sin. Yet Jesus said that the truth would make us free (John 8:32). In another sense, Go does want everything to do with us because He loved us (John 3:16). God provided the means and tools (Bible Teaching) necessary for us to make the right choice of obedience resulting in salvation from our past sins (2 Peter 1:3). Now that our sins are washed away, we can begin a relationship with God. Before we obeyed the gospel we had sin in our life, and God does not tolerate sin in any form or fashion. So now, having our sins removed, we can begin a relationship with God.

The second salvation that is mentioned is the removal of our present sins. This is necessary because we all make mistakes, boo-boo's, errors, or anything that is considered a transgression of God's laws. In other words, sin. Somewhere along the line of not being perfect as we are supposed to try to be, we can lose our relationship with God once again. This is because God does not tolerate anything that defiles, or anything that is sinful. When we realize that we have sinned before God, and His grace and mercy have been removed from us, we have the privilege to confess our sins and ask God for forgiveness. We do not need to be baptized again to have our sins removed. 1 John 1:9 tells us that if we confess our sins, He is faithful and just to forgive our sins. God is more than willing to forgive us our sins, and Christ plays a big part in that forgiveness. It is only through the sacrifice of Christ that this happens (1 John 1:7). So, now, we can return to God and have a relationship with Him once again. Now if we can continue serving God through our obedience and accepting the terms of His grace, we will eventually experience the third salvation.

The third salvation is the part that comes after judgment day. The only part of this that comes to us before judgment is the hope we have through the gospel and our obedience coupled with the promise of eternal life. The righteous will be welcomed into heaven to sit around the throne of God, and worship Him forever. We will dine at His table because of His invitation. That invitation is only offered to the righteous. Those not righteous will be told to depart into everlasting darkness, torment, destruction, and the absence of God. This place is called hell. It is this third salvation in which we strive every day to be pleasing to God in order to be invited into the abode of God called heaven. While we are all looking for the ultimate salvation of spending eternal life in heaven with God, we must realize that is only the result of the third salvation.

Some false teaching that takes place teaches that this third salvation is given at the first response of the gospel. Have you heard of the "once saved, always saved" doctrine? That is a false doctrine that is accepted by millions of people. We are cleansed of our sins and we enter a relationship with God, but the eternal life does not happen then. Only after doing the will of God continuously can we receive the salvation associated with eternal life in heaven. There is too much Bible that stands at odds with those who teach this false doctrine.

There are a lot of people who believe that "faith alone" can save and give us this eternal life. This is also a false doctrine. Our lives must be dedicated to serve the Lord diligently until the day we die. Let us seek to keep our lives pure through obedience so we can enter heaven. The Bible tells us how to get there. It is ours to make that choice of serving God, and if we do so, we will enjoy eternal life in heaven.

How To Obtain Eternal Salvation

The simple answer is to turn to the Bible; read and study it, apply it to your life, and do all the commandments God has given you to do. But for most people, such an answer is out of the question. It is because this answer places accountability upon them before God. Many live in such a way that God wants then to live in such a way which they do not want.

This is a list of things by which a person is saved. We are going to take these thoughts from the Bible and realize that there is so much we have to do to obtain eternal salvation. Like we said before, this is not easy and it really puts a burden upon us to try to reach all of these in our lifetime. Thus we have the need to be diligent in serving the Lord. For most people, doing these things will take a lifetime to accomplish. We realize that we may not accomplish everything on this list; but if we are not making an effort to do everything on this list, we can fall short.

The things (factors) which save are simple to understand and do. It does require a lot of effort and discipline. It requires commitment, dedication, and effort. It takes a lifetime to accomplish, and we can never give up or quit, lest we lose what we have gained.

This list is not complete, but should serve as a guide to study. This list does not contain an exhaustive list of the negative commands of what to avoid or refrain from doing. We will examine briefly some things that will keep us out of heaven. The point being that if we are doing something on that list, we need to cease doing it. Use this in your study and learn the ways of God more perfectly. We need to realize that "Not doing" the things on our list are just as hazardous to our soul as by doing those things God has forbidden us to do.

I would imagine that most of the people who read this have never really considered just how much each of these things have a part in their salvation. Whether you can accept it or not, just remember, while these things may seem unimportant right now, you cannot reach heaven if these things are lacking in you.

Many of the things listed are the actions required on your part to receive and keep your salvation. You can have a part in the salvation of others by example, teaching, encouragement, and a host of other actions that you can do. One thing to remember is the fact that you are responsible for your own salvation.

Though some of these things may not seem significant, I am sure you will agree that we cannot have salvation without them in our lives. We should never give up trying to be saved. We should never be complacent about our salvation. Remember diligence (Hebrews 11:6).

You must remember that it is your choice to do these things. If a person is to benefit from any of this, they must accept it and apply it to their lives.

When Paul told the Philippians to "Work out your own salvation, with fear and trembling" in Philippians 2:12; he meant that he could not do it for them. They would have to do so themselves, in a collective sense.

Each of us, however, will stand before God to give an account for our individual actions and faith (Galatians 6:7-8). No one will stand in your place.

I am going to limit my comments in this section. I will offer a necessary action that one must do along with a few verses that you can look up in your own Bible. Be sure to read the passages in your Bible in their proper context. If you are serious about Bible study, you will realize that most of these things are offered as commands, and not suggestions. In fact there are very few suggestions in God's word.

We should never give up trying to be saved. We should never be complacent about our salvation. Remember that salvation is not easy, but it is simple to understand if you are spiritually minded. If you are not spiritually minded, these will be a problem for you.

God is glorified by his saved ones. Will you be one of them?

A List Of Things By Which Factor Into Our Salvation?

We will first list the things associated with God as it relates to our salvation. Without God there is no salvation, so He is on this list. Without the sacrifice of Jesus, there is no salvation. Without the words of the Holy Spirit to direct us in our actions, there can be no salvation. Obviously God, Christ and the Holy Spirit which we will reference as Deity are crucial for our salvation. Also crucial for our salvation is what they did for us.

This list gives us the Persons and actions of Deity and what They have provided for us.

God:
John 8:41: John 17:3; Acts 5:29; Acts 10:34; Hebrews 12:29; Genesis 1:1
God is described as the Father of the Godhead. The entire knowledge of the universe is in the mind of God. Omniscient (all knowing), Omnipotent (all powerful), Omnipresent (everywhere).

Christ:
Matthew 1:21; John 10:9; John 11:25; 1 Timothy 1:15; John 6:35,41,48,51;John 8:12; John 14:6
The Son of God in which all authority rests until the end. He is our Savior and King. We read in John 21:25 these words: "And there are also many other things which Jesus did, which if they were written in detail, I suppose the even the world itself would not contain the books which were written" (NASV).

Holy Spirit:
Romans 5:5; Romans 14:17; Romans 15:16; 1 Corinthians 6:19; 1 Thessalonians1:5;
The Spirit of God given the charge to make known the Father's and the Son's will to all mankind.

Grace:
John 1:14,17;Romans 3:24; Galatians 1:6,15; Ephesians 1:7;Ephesians 2:5-8; Titus 3:7; 1 Peter 3:7; 2 Peter 3:18
God's part in man's redemption.

Gift of God:
Acts 2:38; Romans 5:15-18; Romans 6:23; Ephesians 2:8;Ephesians 4:7; Hebrews 6:4
This is associated with God's grace. The thing about a gift is that though you do not pay for it, you still must accept it for it to be yours. Sometimes there are conditions placed upon someone in order to receive that gift. Most of God's blessings are conditional upon our actions.

Gospel:
Romans 1:16; 1 Corinthians 15:1-4; Romans 15:16,29; Ephesians 1:13;2 Timothy 1:10;

Romans 10:15; 1 Corinthians 9:16;
This is the good news of salvation that is offered to all mankind. This is the teaching about the grace of God and how to receive it.

Blood of Jesus:
Acts 20:28; Romans 5:9; Ephesians 1:7; 1 Peter 1:18-19:Hebrews 10:19; 1 John 1:7
The blood represents the life of Jesus and the shedding of His blood on our behalf. It is accessed initially by baptism, then received by appeal (prayer) coupled with our repentance and confession.

Book Of Life (Names written In):
Revelation 20:12-15; Revelation 21:27
If our name is written in it, we have done what we were supposed to do. God keeps records of all people. The wicked are written down and the righteous are written down in the books that will be opened on judgment day.

Church:
Acts 2:47; Ephesians 1:22; Ephesians 3:10; Ephesians 5;24; Colossians 1:18
The church is the body of Christ. It is the institution that God appointed to make known the gospel to all mankind.

Discipline:
Hebrews 12:5-13
God does discipline or chastise us. We also have a duty to discipline an unruly member. And yes, we should discipline ourselves.

Forgiveness:
Ephesians 1:7; Colossians 2:13; 1 John 2:12; Colossians 1:14
Only God can offer forgiveness of sins concerning our soul. . If we do our part, God will forgive. God also teaches us to forgive those who have hurt or wronged us. If God does it for us, we should do it to others.

Head:
Ephesians 1:22; Ephesians 4:15; Colossians 1:18
Jesus Christ is head of the church and also head of the body which is His church.

Inheritance:
Colossians 1:12; Colossians 3:24; Hebrews 9:15; 1 Peter 1:4;
Ephesians 1:11
This is what God provides for us. It is ours to receive and also our choice to reject.

Intercession:
Romans 8:26-27,34; Hebrews 11:2

The Holy Spirit does this and Christ also does this for the saints. This means a go-between to bring both parties to a fair conclusion.

Justified:
Romans 3:28; Romans 5:1; 1 Corinthians 6:11; Galatians 2:16; Galatians 3:11; James 2:24,25
Obviously God is the one who justifies us to make us clean in His sight. But we have to obey God in order to be justified.

Light:
John 1:4,7,8,9; 1 Corinthians 4:5; Ephesians 5:8; Colossians 1:12; 1 Peter 2:9; 1 John 1:5,7
Jesus is the true light. Light often represents enlightenment and understanding. The light represents purity and is opposite of darkness which means evil, ignorance, and sin. We must come to the true light in order to be saved.

Purpose Of God:
Ephesians 1:11; Ephesians 3:11; 2 Timothy 1:9
God had His plan of salvation from the beginning. Everything God has done was to bring this plan to completion. You could say that the eternal purpose of God is to save souls. Everything God does for mankind is done for that purpose.

Reconciliation:
Ephesians 2:16; Colossians 1:20; Romans 5:10; 2 Corinthians 5:18,20; Colossians 1:21-22
We are brought back into a relationship with God by His grace and our actions of obedience. Remember our sins separated us from God (Isaiah 59:2), and Jesus provided the sacrifice whereby we can once again be in a relationship with God.

Redemption:
Romans 3:24; Romans 8:23; 1 Corinthians 1:30; Ephesians 1:7,14; Colossians 1:14
Similar to reconciliation. This means to buy back what was lost or given away. In this case our soul was lost in sin, and Jesus paid the price to buy our souls back from Satan.

Remission Of Sins:
Matthew 26:28; Luke 24:47; Acts 2:38; Acts 10:43; Hebrews 9;22; Hebrews 10:18
This is what God will do for us, and we cannot have a relationship with God as long as we have sins. This does not come automatically. It only happens after we have obeyed God's commands by obedient faith.

Resurrection:
John 11:25; Romans 1:4; 1 Corinthians 15:3-4; Philippians 3:10; 1 Peter 1:3;

1 Peter 3:21; Revelation 20:5-6

This is what Jesus did, and is the very foundation of the gospel. Without this, no promise of God could be trusted.

Revelation:

Romans 16:25; Galatians 1:12; Ephesians 1:17; Ephesians 3:3; 1 Peter 1:13

God's revealed will to mankind. Also the appearance of God to mankind in the person of Jesus is called a revelation. This revealing has been made known to us through the Bible.

Reward:

1 Corinthians 3:8; Hebrews 11:6; Revelation 2:10

God will reward us for our faithfulness, and if we are faithful until the end, God will reward us with the best ever.

Sanctified:

1 Corinthians 1:30; 1 Thessalonians 4:3,4; 1 Peter 1:2; 1 Corinthians 1:2; Ephesians 5:26; 1 Peter 3:15

This is what God does for us after we have been obedient to His commands. The word means "set apart for a purpose". We are set apart from the world that we might be an example to the world. We are set apart to do God's will and purpose.

Scripture:

2 Timothy 3:16-17; 2 Peter 1:20; Romans 15:4; Romans 16:26; 1 Corinthians 15:3-4; 2 Timothy 3:15

This is what the Holy Spirit has given us. If we follow it to the best of our ability, our result will be eternal life in heaven. Can we ignore scripture and still go to heaven?

Seal:

2 Timothy 2:19; 2 Corinthians 1:22; Ephesians 1:13; Ephesians 4:30

The Holy Spirit places a seal of approval upon us. This is like a surety or guarantee that confirms we meet the qualifications to be called Christians. Most professionals will display their seal of approval so that they can do what they are doing. We call this a diploma. But we must remember this seal only last as long as we are faithful to God in all things.

Testator:

Hebrews 9:16-17

This has reference to Jesus. It is like having a last will and testament being read. In this case, Jesus, the testator did give us His will, and it is our job to fulfill that will.

Translated:

Colossians 1:13

This means a changing in location or condition. Jesus changed Christians from sinners to saints and put us into His kingdom where they previously had not been. In Acts 2:47 where it says the Lord added to their number daily, he mentions the condition that had been changed; those who were being saved.

Wash:
Acts 22:16; 1 Corinthians 6:11; Hebrews 10:22; Titus 3:5
God washes away our sins when we are baptized. This is the cleansing that must occur for us to be worthy to enter that most holy place where God dwells. God took away our sins when we obeyed the gospel. Titus calls this the washing of regeneration.
2 Corinthians 5:17 tells us that if we are in Christ we are a new creature. Romans 6:4 tells us that we arise from baptism to walk in newness of life. God also reveals that if we walk in the light of God, the blood of Jesus cleanses us from sin (1 John 1:7)

Will Of God:
2 Corinthians 8:5; Romans 12:2; Galatians 1:4; Ephesians 6:6; Colossians 4:12;
1 Thessalonians 4:3; 1 John 2:17
This is what God wants, and we must do His will.

The Word of God (The Bible):
Psalm 119:160; John 17:17; 2 Timothy 4:2
The Bible is God's revealed word to mankind and should be treated with respect and obedience.

A List Of Things By Which A Person Is Saved?

Some of these are your personal actions required of you. Some of these things are what you are supposed to be. Some of these things are what you are supposed to do.

Abiding :
John 15:1-10; Romans 8:1; 2 Corinthians 5:17; 1John 5:12; 2John 9
This means to dwell, stay, live, and remain within the guidelines set up by God. Abiding in the doctrine means to not add to nor take away from the teaching of God.

Abhor Evil:
Romans 12:9
God hates evil, and so should we.

Ability:
Romans 4:21; 1 Corinthians 10:13; Ephesians 3:18; Ephesians 6:11 2 Timothy 2:2
God gives us ability, and we should learn to nurture and grow our ability, because He has a plan to use us to help others. Everyone has an ability of one kind or another. Learn what your ability is and use it, don't sit on it.

Abstain:
1 Thessalonians 4:3; 1 Thessalonians 5:22; 1 Peter 2:11
If you cannot keep away from evil, how can you remain with God?

Add To Your Faith:
2 Peter 1:5
Adding virtue, knowledge, temperance, patience, godliness, brotherly kindness, and love. It is the process of growing and maturing into a godly Christian.

Approved:
Romans 14:18; 1 Corinthians 11:19; 2 Timothy 2:15
In order to be approved of God, we must do something. Doing nothing will not gain His approval.

Arise:
Acts22:16; Ephesians 5:14
While Christ arose, we must arise from laziness or inaction to do what God wants us to do.

Assembling With The Saints:
Hebrews 10:25; Acts 20:7
The greatest people on earth are the saints, so why would you not want to spend time with them. In reality, they are the only people on earth who care for your soul and want you to go to heaven with them.

Attain:
Philippians 3:11
We have to reach up to a higher standard and calling. If we do not make any effort, how can we reach heaven?

Awake:
Romans 13:11; 1Corinthians 15:34
Wake up and pay attention to what is going on around you.

Baptism:
Mark 16:16; Acts 2:38; Acts 22:16; Romans 6:3-6; Galatians 3:26-27; 1 Peter 3:21
Baptism is rejected by most of the error of many religions. If there is any must do thing to bring about salvation this ranks up there as one of the more important and essential things. Baptism is what puts us into Christ and His church. Baptism is what removes sins. The bible emphasizes the necessity of baptism, and many people reject its essential nature.

Bear Fruit:
Mark 4:20; John 15:2,5,16
This is done in several ways. The example we set will do this. The teaching of others will do this. The defense of the truth will do this. Helping others see the light of Jesus and teaching them to do what God commands will be the fruit we bear. Just remember in the parables of Jesus that plants that did not bear fruit were cast into the fire.

Bear one another's burdens:
Galatians 6:2
The importance of letting your brethren help you and you helping others.

Believing:
John 3:16; John 8:24; John 20:31; Acts 16:31; Ephesians 2:8-9
This is faith. The implication is that faith alone does not save, but faith working with our actions that demonstrate this faith will save.

Boldness:
Acts 4:31; Ephesians 3:12; Philippians 1:20; 1John 4:17
God's word is so powerful, we should feed off of His power and present the message with confidence.

Born Again:
John 3:3,5,7; 1Peter 1:23
This is what happens in baptism.

Buffet:
1Corinthians 9:27
Control your body. And it does not hurt to control your thoughts or your tongue.

Calling On The Lord:
Acts 2:21, Acts 22:16; Philippians 3:14;
This is more than using the mouth to call out to God. This is in effect an appeal to God and backing up that appeal with obedience and reverence.

Childbearing (women only):
1 Timothy 2:15
I do not subscribe to the idea that a woman must bear a child in order to be saved. Some have taught this over the years and there are a lot of problems associated with such teaching.

Cleave,Cling:
Romans 12:9
Hang on to that which is good as described by God. Don't let go of the truth.

Commands (this is what you are to obey):
Matthew 28:20; John 15:14; Acts 20:48; 1 Corinthians 7:19; 1 John 3:24
This is what God expects from everyone. If we obey His commands, He will be pleased with us. You cannot ignore or refuse the commands and expect to go to heaven. Sadly some teach that very thing and such is false doctrine.

Communion:
1Corinthians 10:16
While we commune with the saints, we are also communing with Jesus and God.

Compassion:
1 Peter 3:8; Matthew 18:33; Colossians 3:12
This was a quality of Jesus, and we are supposed to learn to be like Jesus. If you do not have compassion, you will never make an effort to save someone who is lost.

Confession:
Romans 10:9-10; Acts 8:35-37
Good for the soul. We acknowledge our faith in Jesus before our baptism. And we also make the declaration to the world that Jesus is Our Lord and Savior. This we should be willing to do the rest of our lives.

Conscience (not violated):
Romans 14:23; 1Timothy 1:5,19
If you do something that violates your conscience, you are sinning before God. If your gut tells you not to do something, listen and play it safe.

Contend:
Jude 3
Sometimes we have to take up the fight for God's rights. There are many false teachers in the world, and somebody has to speak up to defend the truth.

Continue In The Faith:
John 8:31; John 15:9; Acts 13:43; Acts 14:22; Colossians 1:23; 1John 2:24;
2Timothy 3:14
Remember, this is a lifelong effort on our part.

Contribution:
Romans 15:26; 1Corinthians 16:2
We can contribute our funds to support the local church and assist those in need. But
we can also contribute of ourselves to benefit the church.

Conversation (manner of life):
Philippians 1:27; Philippians 3:20; Hebrews 13:5; 1 Peter 1:15; 1Peter 3:1-2
One of the words from the King James version that has evolved over the years to mean
something different than when originally used.

Conversion:
Matthew 13:15; Mark 4:12; Matthew 18:3; John 12:40; Acts 3:19; James 5:19
This just means a change has taken place.

Counsel:
Acts 20:27
All of God's word is described as His counsel.

Death (symbolic):
Romans 6:3-5,9; 1Corinthians 11:26; Philippians 2:8; Hebrews 2:9,14; Hebrews 9:16;
Revelation 2:10
We must put off our old self which is dead to God and do the actions to bring a new life.
This is initially accomplished in baptism which is the symbol of the death, burial, and
resurrection of Jesus.

Deeds:
Romans 15:18; Romans 2:6;
We will be judged by our deeds, so we better make sure we are doing the right things.

Diligence:
Hebrews 11:6; Ephesians 4:3; 2 Peter 1:5,10; Jude3; Hebrews 4:11
Means to make every effort. The idea in scripture is to become very passionate about
our duty to obey God and teach others.

Discern:
Hebrews 5;14; 1Corinthians 11:29
Pay attention to what is going on and think carefully on what we are doing. Focus on
the right thing, and anything not right should become evident when we encounter it.

Discipline:
Hebrews 12:5-13
Yes God disciplines us, but we also have to discipline others who become unruly.

Doing:
Matthew 7:21; James 1:19-24
Jesus was so plain here. Nobody will get to heaven unless they do God's will. How hard is this to understand?

Draw Near To God:
John 6:44; John 12:32; Hebrews 10:22; Hebrews 7:19; James 4:8
When we make the effort to get closer to God, God will make sure He is available to us.

Drink:
John 4:13-14; 1 Corinthians 11:26-29
This is symbolic language which means to take in.

Dying To The Sinful Life (a.k.a. death)
Romans 6:12,13,16; Colossians 3:5-7
Our old self of sin must be put away from us. We have to determine to not do those things which we used to do.

Eat:
1 Corinthians 11:26-29; John 6:53-58
Same as drink. Symbolic language meaning to take in. Also carries the idea of communion with Christ.

Edification:
Romans 15:2; 1 Corinthians 14:3; 2 Corinthians 10:8;Romans 14:9;
1 Thessalonians 5:11; 1 Corinthians 14:26; Ephesians 4:12,26,29
What we receive in the form of education and encouragement. Also what we do for others to help them grow.

Election:
Romans 9:11; Romans 11:5-7; Matthew 24:31; Colossians 3:12; 2 Peter 1:10
We are the elect or chosen of God. We receive this status when we obey Him.

Encouragement:
Philippians 4:8; Hebrews 11:25
Similar to edification. Everybody needs this from others.

Endure:
Matthew 24:13; Mark 13:13; 2 Timothy 2:10; James 5:11; Hebrews 12:2-3; Hebrews 10:22
Hang in there. In the end it will all be worth it.

Enlightened:
Ephesians 1:18; Hebrews 6:4
We need to learn things. The word is described in such a way as it is to turn the lights on. Without light, there is confusion and you are not really sure what is taking place. But when the light comes on, you can see clearly and make good decisions. Plus you will be safer. Enlightened means to open the windows of your mind.

Enters In:
Matthew 7:21; Matthew 7:13; Matthew 19:24; Matthew 25:21; Hebrews 4:11; Hebrews 10:19; John 10:1-2
This actually takes us to judgment day where we will enter into heaven. Sure we have to be invited, but we must also remember that no unqualified person shall enter in. Only those who have met God's requirements will enter into heaven.

Entertain:
Hebrews 13:2
This should be seen as hospitality rather than entertainment.

Entrance:
2 Peter 1:11
We are supposed to secure our entrance into heaven. We do this by being obedient.

Equipped:
2 Timothy 3:17; Ephesians 4:12
God gives us the tools we need to be faithful and grow. If we throw away the tools we will be unprepared and ill prepared for the task before us, and we will be marked as unworthy.

Escape:
1 Corinthians 10:13; Hebrews 12:25; 2 Peter 1:4
We escape the snare of Satan when we turn and practice the truth.

Establish:
Romans 1:11; Colossians 2:7;
This is the same as taking a stand, or being grounded or rooted. It means we will not waver when the tempter comes.

Evangelize; Evangelist:
2 Timothy 4:5; Ephesians 4:11; Romans 10:14-15
Share the gospel message. Declare to all what God has done for mankind.

Examine:
Galatians 6:4; 2 Corinthians 13:5; 1 John 4:1
Testing yourself to see if you are faithful, and testing what we are taught as compared to the truth of God's word.

Examples:
1 Corinthians 10:11; 2 Thessalonians 3:9; 1 Peter 5:3; 1 Timothy 4:12
We must be examples to others. If we are not doing anything for Christ, we cannot be an example of faithfulness or of being a Christian.

Exceed:
Matthew 5:20
We need to be better than the Pharisees who considered themselves the most righteous people on earth at that time.

Excel:
1 Corinthians 14:12
We need to be better

Excellence:
Philippians 4:8
This is what we are to strive for.

Exercise:
Hebrews 5:14; Hebrews 12:11; 2 Peter 2:14
Bodily exercise helps our overall health, Spiritual exercise helps our souls.

Exhortation:
1 Thessalonians 4:1; 1 Thessalonians 5:14; 1 Timothy 2:1; 1 Timothy 6:2;
Hebrews 3:13; 1 Timothy 4:13; Hebrews 10:25
We know and learn just how important our brethren in Christ can be. We need to encourage others, and hopefully we are encouraged by others. Think of exhortation as a sort of pep rally.

Faith:
Hebrews 11:1,6; Romans 5:1; Ephesians 2:8-9; Romans 10:14; Romans 1:5; Romans 4:5,9,11-16; Romans 14:23; Galatians 3:7,9; 1 Timothy 6:12; 2 Timothy 4:7;
James 2:14-26; Jude 3
This faith is not limited to a mental declaration of belief, but is a response to God's grace. This faith needs to be strong enough to withstand challenges to your belief. This faith should cause you to be obedient to all of what God commands through His word.

Fearing God:
Ecclesiastes 12:13; 1 Timothy 5:20; Matthew 10:28; Acts 10:35
This means a form of reverence towards God. Of course, if you are not living right, you should fear God.

Fellowship:
1 Corinthians 1:9; 1 Corinthians 10:20; Philippians 1:5; Philippians 2:1;
1 John 1: 3, 6,7
Means having a relationship. The Greek word (koinonia) means "to share" or have things in common. We enjoy fellowship when we share a meal or come together to worship God.

Fervent:
Romans 12:11; James 5:16; 1 Peter 4:8; 1 Peter 1:22
This gives us the idea of being passionate about what we are doing.

Fight The Good Fight:
1 Timothy 6:12; 2 Timothy 4:7
Fighting for no reason is evil. Fighting for a cause can be noble or stupid depending upon what cause you are fighting for. Standing up for the truth is a good fight. Standing up for anything condemned in the Bible is stupid and puts you at odds against God.

Flee:
1 Thessalonians 5:22; 1 Corinthians 6:18; 1 Corinthians 10:14; 2 Timothy 2:22
Get away from sin as fast as you can. God gives you the ability to resist evil, and you better resist it. Do not take chances thinking you can withstand it.

Follow:
1 Thessalonians 5:15; 2 Thessalonians 3:9; 1 Peter 2:21; John 10:14; Matthew 16:24; John 10:27; John 12:26
Jesus is the One we are to follow. The teaching of Jesus (His word) is what we are to follow. In this case, follow means to stay within the guidelines God has given us.

Forgiving Others:
Matthew 6:12,14,15; Matthew 18:21-35; Luke 17:3-4
Our duty towards man.

Forgiveness:
Ephesians 1:7; Colossians 2:13; 1 John 2:12; Colossians 1:14
God forgives sins. We also should have an attitude of forgiveness towards others.

Freedom From Sins:
 John 8:32; Romans 6:18,22; Galatians 5:1
When we are obedient, we are justified and cleansed from our sins. Thus we have freedom from sin.

Fulfill:
James 2:8; Philippians 2:2; Galatians 6:2
More like complete your task whether it be a specific task or a general task of demonstrating your faith to others.

Gentleness:
Galatians 5:22; Galatians 6:1
Not weak by any means. This idea might include nurturing or feeding. In this case teaching someone what God expects of them. It also includes being nice or kind when such would normally be unexpected.

Giving:
1 Corinthians 7:5; Romans 12:19; 1 Timothy 4:13; Hebrews 2:1; 2 Peter 1:5
We give to God by our contribution; but we also give of ourselves to others and to the cause of Christ.

Glorifying God:
Matthew 5:16; John 12:28; Romans 15:6,9; 1 Peter 4:11
Everything we do should be for this purpose.

Going:
Hebrews 6:1; Mark 16:15
Go preach the gospel. Go do those things God wants you to do.

Godliness:
1 Timothy 2:2,10; 1 Timothy 4:7; 2 Peter 1:6-7;
This should be a character trait that others would honor us for being. Living your life as if God is the most important thing is included in this trait.

Godly:
2 Corinthians 7:10; 2 Timothy 3:12; Titus 2:12; Hebrews 12:28;
So similar to Godliness. We should become the type of people with character traits that are usually reserved for God. Things like love, care, compassion, tender-hearted and so forth.

Good Works:
Matthew 5:16; Ephesians 2:10; 1 Timothy 2:10; 1 Timothy 6:18; Titus 2:7;
Hebrews 10:24; 1 Peter 2:12
God tells us what good works He wants us to do. If we do not do good works, we will not enter heaven.

Goodness:
Galatians 5:22; Romans 11:22; Romans 15:14; Ephesians 5:9
Just an overall aura about us in which people can call us good.

Grounded (Foundation, or Firmly Rooted, or Established):
Ephesians 3:7; Colossians 1:23
If you have no foundation, your faith is weak. Also consider the foolish man who built his house on the sand.

Growth:
Ephesians 4:15; 1 Peter 2:2; 2 Peter 3:18; Ephesians 2:21; 2 Thessalonians 1:3
If you are not growing, you are stagnant and dying. You are either growing or you are digressing. There is no middle ground whereby you may coast along. Uphill or downhill are your only possible directions. It seems that many people treat this command as a suggestion or option. While we do have the option to grow or not, God wants us to grow, so when we fail to grow, we are not pleasing to God. Anyone who does not please God will not make it to heaven.

Guidance:
Acts 8:31; John 16:13
Follow the instruction and teaching in God's word, and help others along the way.

Handling Accurately:
2 Timothy 2:15
What we do with what we have. This especially applies to our Bible study.

Hearing:
Matthew 15:10; Romans 10:14-15; Romans 10:17; 1 Timothy 4:16; James 1:19; Revelation 1:3; Acts 2:37; Acts 4:4; Acts 5:5; 2 Timothy 2:2; Matthew 7:24; John 9:31; James 1:22,23,25
The implication and inference is that one hears so as to obey.

Hold Fast:
1 Thessalonians 5:21; Hebrews 3:6; 2 Timothy 1:13; Hebrews 4-14;
If you find the truth, hold on to it and do not waver in your faith.

Holiness:
Romans 1:14; Romans 6:19,22; 2 Corinthians 7: 1; 1 Thessalonians 3:13; 1 Timothy 2:15; Titus 2:3; Hebrews 12:10
Usually associated with God or the things of God. This character trait is something we need to become in our own lives

Honesty:
1 Timothy 2:2; 2 Corinthians 13:7
Can you really think that a dishonest person is acceptable to God? Then make sure you have integrity and treat others fairly.

Hope:
Acts 2:26; Romans 5:2; Romans 12:12; Romans 15:13; Titus 1:2; Philippians 1:20; Colossians 1:5,23,27; Titus 2:13; Hebrews 3:7
This gives us a great motivator. The fact that we can see what all this religious stuff does for us, and because we are faithful, we can have that hope.

Hospitality:
Romans 12:13; 1 Peter 4:9
Seeing a need in others and acting to correct or fix that need.

Humility:
James 4:10; 1 Peter 5:6; 1 Peter 5:5; Luke 14:11; Romans 12:3;
Philippians 2:3-4
So often mentioned in the scripture that one would be hard pressed to find a proud person suitable for God. Perhaps in their own eyes, but not in God's eyes.

Hunger:
Matthew 5:6; Luke 6:21; John 6:35; Revelation 7:16
Just like we might crave physical food when we have been deprived of it, so also we should crave the word of God knowing that such will feed our soul.

I (yourself):
1 Corinthians 11:1; Galatians 2:19-20
While I do have a part in my salvation, I realize that I am important to God. I am also important to others. All of this is conditional upon my obedience to God and my service to others. Most of the time, the "I" gets in the way of submission and humility. That is what we call pride, and we must not think of ourselves more highly than others.

Increasing:
2 Peter 1:5-11
This is concerning our growth in our faith. It is a continuous process of constant growth.

Joint-heirs:
Romans 8:17
We are blessed with the privilege of going to heaven. God treats us as His children and just as Jesus is an heir of God, so we can be also. We do this by our obedience to His word.

Joy:
Galatians 5:22; Philippians 2:1,2
This should be a catalyst to motivate us to be pleasing to God. Not only that, but we should spread joy around wherever we go.

Keeping:
1 Corinthians 9:27; 1 Corinthians 11:2; 1 Corinthians 15:2; Ephesians 4:3;
1 Timothy 6:20; James 1:27
Holding and doing the commandments of God. His commandments are not a onetime good enough thing, but a lifetime continuous effort on our part.

Kindness:
Ephesians 2:7; Colossians 3:12; 2 Peter 1:7
We are commanded to be kind to everyone. If you are not kind to others, what makes you think that God will show His kindness to you? Something to think about!

Knowledge:
Romans 11:33; Colossians 1:10; 2 Peter 1:2,3,5,8; 2 Peter 2:20; 2 Peter 3:18;
2 Corinthians 4:6; 1 Timothy 2:4; Romans 9:22,23; Ephesians 6:19; Colossians 1:27
This understanding we acquire is so important. We learn what God expects from us and we apply such knowledge to our lives. We also should be willing to share our knowledge of God as Paul did in Ephesians 3:3-4.

Labour:
1 Corinthians 3:8; 1 Thessalonians 1:3; Revelation 2:2,3; 1 Timothy 5:8;
Philippians 4:3; Revelation 14:3
We must work to obtain salvation and eternal life. It does not come about if we are lazy.

Law:
Romans 7:21-25; Romans 13:10; James 1:25; James 2:8; 1 John 3:4;
2 Timothy 2:5
Sometimes the Law has reference to the covenant that Moses gave the people. This law is important because it is the schoolmaster that teaches people about the Christ who was to come (Galatians 3:24). Since Christ died on the cross, we live under a new law. Many people fail to see that the system of Grace has its own law that we are subject to.

Lay up:
Matthew 6:19-20; 2 Timothy 4:8
Put away, make a deposit, purchase a ticket, be prepared. So many ways to describe what this means.

Learn:
Matthew 11:29; 1 Corinthians 4:6; 1 Corinthians 14:31; Philippians 4:9; Romans 15:4
How can one develop without learning?

Leaving The Elementary:
Hebrews 6:1
By implication, growth is necessary. The Hebrew writer chastised Christians that did not grow.

Loseth:
Matthew 10:39
Speaking of humility, one must forfeit their own desires and put God first. Many are not willing to do this, yet still expect to get to heaven; that will not happen.

Love:
Romans 8:35; John 15:13; Romans 12:9,10; Galatians 5:6,22; Philippians 1:9; Philippians 2:1-2; Hebrews 10:24; 1 John 4:7-18; John 15:12,17
The greatest command of all is love. If we cannot love, we cannot go to heaven.

Lovingkindness:
Romans 2:4
A character trait that we should always exhibit in our lives.

Lowliness (of mind):
Ephesians 4:2; Philippians 2:3
Humility.

Mercy:
Titus 3:5; 1 Peter 1:3
While God provides His mercy, we must also show mercy to others.

Milk:
1 Corinthians 3:2; 1 Peter 2:2
As a newborn baby cannot digest or eat meat, they must start at the beginning drinking milk. As they grow (just like a Christian is supposed to do) they will become more mature and be able to handle meat or more complicated issues.

Minister, Ministry:
1 Timothy 4:6; 1 Peter 1:12
Taking care of other's needs. This word is better understood as serving or servitude. We have a ministry to fulfill by providing the best service we can offer to anyone. Teaching people about God and salvation is the very best you can do for anyone. On occasion, this teaching ministry needs to be accompanied by a ministry of service.

Moderation:
Philippians 4:5
Too much of a good thing can be bad. Even Paul told Timothy to drink a little wine (not necessarily an alcoholic beverage) for his health. We are not to be seen as excessive in things we do, and we are not to make a spectacle of ourselves either.

Modesty:
1 Timothy 2:9
While most people apply this to what we wear, both men and women, the understanding of the scripture is focused upon our behavior. Yes, our dress does say a lot about us. Look to see how the world views various types of clothing.

Name:
Colossians 3:17; Ephesians 1:21; Matthew 28:29; Acts 4:7,12; Philippians 4:3
In this case. this means doing things by the authority of Christ or God. There is no salvation in any other name.

Narrow Way:
Matthew 7:14
This is where we need to strive to be because the broad way leads to destruction.

Nobleminded:
Acts 17:11
Notice that this was a compliment and serves as an example that we should study the scriptures daily to verify what we have been taught.

Nourishment:
Ephesians 5:29; James 5:5; 1 Timothy 4:6; Colossians 2:19
A reference to our spiritual food which includes Bible study and encouragement from the saints.

Nurture:
Ephesians 6:4
We must be nurtured by training. We also can nurture those less mature than we are.

Obedience:
Matthew 7:21; Matthew 21-28-31; Romans 2:8-9; Philippians 2:12; Hebrews 5:9
One cannot get to heaven unless they are obedient to the commands of God.

Observe:
1 Timothy 5:21
Pay attention.

Obtain:
Romans 11:31; 1 Corinthians 9;24; 1 Thessalonians 5:9; 1 Timothy 2:10
Get it and hang on to it.

One:
Ephesians 4:4-6; Romans 5:15-19; John 17:11,21,22,23
The ones are important. There is one way to heaven, and that is by doing what God commands us to do. There is only one church that is acceptable to God. There is only one faith that God recognizes. There is one Lord and one type of baptism. Recognizing the ones of God is vital to our salvation.

Opportunity:
Galatians 6:10; Hebrews 11:15
We all have opportunity all the time. What we need to do is develop ourselves to see these opportunities and respond.

Oracles:
1 Peter 4:11; Romans 3:2; Hebrews 5:12
The messages or teachings that come from God. We are to proclaim the message of God in the same way as He commanded those messages.

Overcome:
Romans 12:21; 1 John 2:13; Revelation 2:7,11,17,26; Revelation 3:5,12,21
To become victorious. This happens when we resist the temptations and stay with God and do what He says.

Parents:
Ephesians 6:1; Colossians 3:20
Some people are blessed to have had faithful parents that taught them the ways of God. Parents have a great responsibility with the souls of their children. Sadly many parents do not teach their children respect for God or others.

Partaking:
1 Corinthians 9:10; 1 Peter 5:1; Romans 15:27; Colossians 1:12; Hebrews 3:1,14; 2 Peter 1:4
Sharing with others in our faith, our resources and our talents. We could also say that partaking is like taking it all in and focusing upon the big picture.

Pastors (Elders):
1 Peter 5:1-3; James 5:14
They watch out for your soul, and these experienced Christians can set a good example for you.

Pattern:
1 Timothy 1:16; Titus 2:7
Some people question whether there is a pattern we should follow. Most people who do this do not want to follow the Bible and its teachings.

Peace:
Philippians 4:7; Colossians 3:15; Galatians 5:22; Ephesians 4;3; 1 Thessalonians 5:13
Getting along with others, and in a way, getting along with yourself.

Perceive:
1 John 3:16
Looking and studying to understand is what is meant by the message being presented.

Perfection:
James 1:4,17,25; James 2:22; Matthew 5:48; Romans 2:12; Philippians 3:12-14; Hebrews 6:1
Spiritual maturity is what is often meant when this word is used. Perfection should be our goal even though we realize we will not walk on water or do some of the things Jesus did.

Persecutions:
Romans 12:14; 1 Corinthians 4:12; Acts 8:1,4; 2 Timothy 3:12
We must stand strong in our faith because those of the world will make trouble for us. This may come in the form of mocking, ridicule, and even hatred. The scriptures teach us that while persecution may be uncomfortable, it can make us stronger Christians.

Perseverance:
Ephesians 6:18;
(see Endurance)

Persuasion:
2 Corinthians 5:11; Acts 18:4; Romans 14:5; Acts 26:28
This can be seen two ways. It means being convinced in your own mind, thus a synonym for faith. In the other sense, we should strive to persuade men to be faithful.

Pleasing God:
1 John 3:22; Philippians 4:18; Colossians 3:20; Hebrews 13:21
That is what it is all about.

Praise:
Philippians 4:8; Acts 16:25
Praise God for sure, but also offer praise to others that are doing good for God.

Prayer:
1 Thessalonians 5:17; 1 Timothy 2:1; Philippians 4:6; Romans 12:12; Colossians 4:2
We could write volumes and not cover it all. Prayer is a privilege that we should never take for granted. We have the opportunity to make requests to the One who can do all things. Your prayer life is an indicator of just how much faith you have. Praying a lot indicates a strong faith. Praying a little indicates weak faith.

Preparation:
Ephesians 6:15
This comes through study and working out our salvation. Always being ready as we see in 1 Peter 3:15.

Present, presentation:
Romans 12:1; Ephesians 5:27
Christ is going to present His bride (the church) to God someday. We can associate this with preparing for an audition or a test. We are going to appear before God someday. We need to present our best.

Press on:
Philippians 3:14
Never give up, never surrender (except to God) should be our motto. And we should strive to move forward in our development of ourselves for serving God.

Priesthood:
1 Peter 2:5,9
We are part of the priesthood of God. We cannot get to heaven unless we are of this priesthood. It is our obedience that puts us into this priesthood. Every child of God is part of this priesthood.

Promise:
Acts 2:33,39; Ephesians 1:13; Hebrews 9:15, Hebrews 10:36; 2 Peter 3:9
Obviously, if you make a promise you should keep it. But we also live by the promise of God, and quite frankly, God has an excellent track record when it comes to keeping promises. So in some ways, the very fact that God made promises, and we believe those promises motivate us to keep doing what God wants us to do because there is a great reward if we do.

Purity:
Philippians 4:8; 1 Timothy 5:22; Hebrews 10:22; 1 John 3:3;2 Corinthians 6:6;
1 Peter 1:22; 1 Timothy 4:12
Free from evil. Can anyone enter heaven who is evil? Of course not! We have our own purity to keep clean and as members of His church, we have an obligation to keep the church pure (free from sin and evil).

Purpose In Your Heart:
Acts 11:23; Ezra 7:10
This should be our desire to learn about God so that we can live like He wants us to live, and grow to the point where we can teach God's law to others. The heart is our mind and directs our every thought, word, and action.

Put On:
Ephesians 6:11; Colossians 3:12: Galatians 3:27
It is like getting dressed for a special occasion. The armor to protect ourselves from Satan, and we clothe ourselves with Christ. This is what we are to become. We are to live this way. This is not something that we put on Sunday morning for church and easily take it off when we leave church.

Quietness:
2 Thessalonians 3:12; 1 Timothy 2:2
Women are to learn in quietness (not ruling over the men) which gives the sense of modest behavior and respectful behavior. But not limited to women in our overall behavior. Sometimes, keeping our tongue still is the wisest thing we can do.

Read:

Ephesians 3:4; Colossians 4:6

For the purpose of obtaining knowledge. Such knowledge can direct our steps and the way we live. We should read to understand. Some people cannot read; it does not mean they will be lost. Most people can at least hear so as to learn. That is what most of the world did many years ago.

Readiness:

Acts 17:11; 2 Corinthians 8:11

Once again, the idea of being prepared.

Receive:

Acts 2:38; Acts 10:43; Romans 5:17; 1 Corinthians 3:14; Galatians 3:14; Galatians 4:5; Colossians 3:24-25

What we receive should be under consideration. We should receive the word of God like the Bereans. We should be willing to receive the lost back into the fold. We should receive brethren into our homes. We should receive every opportunity to learn God's word, and welcome those who want to learn God's word.

Redeeming:

Ephesians 5:16; Colossians 4:5

Making the most of our time as in Ephesians and opportunity in Colossians.

Refrain:

1 Peter 3:10

Some things we just need to back off from. We need to keep ourselves away from evil and sin.

Rejoice:

Romans 12:15; 1 Thessalonians 5:16; Philippians 3:1; Philippians 4:4

We are to rejoice with others. Whether you realize it or not, this is a command. Usually, rejoicing is the result of our blessings. When we are obedient to God, we should know that we have done what makes God happy, and as a result we should rejoice that we have made Him happy. In a way, we should rejoice because we have done that which can help us get to heaven.

Remain:

1 Thessalonians 4:15,17

Hang in there. Do not leave your station. If you are in Christ, you must work to remain in Christ. Remember that Christ dwells in you and He will stay there as long as you purpose to stay in Christ.

Remember:

Acts 20:35; 2 Timothy 2:8; Jude 17; Revelation 2:15; Revelation 3:3; Hebrews 10:17; 1 Corinthians 11:25; 2 Peter 1:13

There are many reasons to remember. We should remember the old paths and seek to walk therein (Jeremiah 6:16). We should remember what we are taught and remain there if what we were taught is the truth. We should remember those souls who have departed from the faith and pray for them. This is not to say we should dwell in the past. In Revelation 3, John said that the Lord remembered their past, but now they have a problem of having left their first love. Too often, we dwell on the past when we may have stood up for the truth, and give ourselves a pat on the back; while in the present, we are doing nothing.

Remove:

Colossians 3:8; Matthew 7:5

The eye if it offends. The hand if it offends. Remove the evil from your life. Remove the one who walks disorderly among you. Remove the log from your eye before you attempt to remove the speck from another's eye.

Renewal:

Colossians 3:10-11; Ephesians 4:23;

We need a constant renewal. Our Christian life is not an easy one sometimes. Paul said that the outward man decays, but the inward man is renewed (2 Corinthians 4:16).

Repent:

Luke 13:3,5; Acts 2:38; 2 Corinthians 7:9,10; 2 Peter 3:9

The meaning of repent is to change direction or course of life. For most people this happens when they realize that they have been living for themselves instead of God. They realize their actions have been in conflict with God's will, and it is time to make a change in their life. This needs to be a noticeable change in the right direction. There are times when we have wronged another, and we must express our sorrow, and determine not to wrong them again.

Reprove:

Ephesians 5:11; 2 Timothy 4:2

This is sometimes necessary when dealing with brethren who are weak in the faith, and who continue to walk disorderly. As teachers, we must reprove those who speak falsehood.

Resist:

James 4:7

We must resist Satan, and not give in to his temptations. We must also resist the urge to do things our way. We should always have the attitude of Jesus when He said: "Not My will, but Thy will".

Restore:
Galatians 6:1
Bring a lost soul back to God. Bring an erring brother back to the fold. In other words, to make things right again, or to bring back to a previous condition. In our case, to bring a child of God back into a relationship with God.

Righteousness:
Titus 2:12; Acts 24:25; Romans 1:17; 2 Corinthians 3:9; Ephesians 5:9; Ephesians 6:14; Philippians 1:11; 2 Timothy 4:8; Romans 4:22; James 2:23
A study of this word reveals much. It sort of reminds us of buying a car. Sure we negotiate the price after we have discussed the dealer fixing minor things. Once we have made the bargain we are happy with, we realize the dealer also is happy with the bargain. Both parties win. The dealer made profit and the customer feels good about a good deal for himself. When we do right by our agreement with God, we are considered righteous. Our part is the obedience commanded by Him through His word, and God's part is providing our eternal home. This can only happen as long as we comply with our agreement.

Rooted:
Ephesians 3;17; Colossians 2:7
If you are not grounded and rooted in the faith, you will fall away. Jesus spoke of the seed that fell on the rocky soil. It sprouted up quickly, but had no firm foundation or it was not rooted. So when tribulation came, it dried up and fell away (Matthew 13:20-21).

Run:
1 Corinthians 9:24,26; Galatians 2:2; Galatians 5:7; Philippians 2:16; Hebrews 12:1
This action verb is used to express the idea that we have to continually grow our service and life to the Lord. We run the race with endurance fixing our gaze upon Jesus. We run according to the rules. We run so as to win. This example used by Paul is like a parable of Jesus. Paul used something which everyone was familiar with, and made a spiritual application out of it.

Sacrifice:
Romans 12:1; Ephesians 5:2; Philippians 4:18; Hebrews 10:12; 1 Peter 2:5
This has reference to what we put into our faith and religion. In the Old Testament God required an animal sacrifice in His worship. We also remember the sacrifice was to be of the best they had. We have to sacrifice a lot of things in order to be a Christian. We must give up our old lifestyle and begin living His lifestyle. Jesus made the ultimate sacrifice for us. Should we not give to God our very best?

Salt:
Matthew 5:13; Colossians 4:6
This speaks of our example that we show others. If you do not show a good example, can you go to heaven?

Searching:
John 5:39; Acts 17:11; 1 Peter 1:10
We are to examine the scriptures carefully. We are to make careful inquiry as to whether what we have been taught is true to God's word or not. We also need to go searching when a lost sheep is out there.

Seeing:
Acts 17:24-25; Colossians 3:9; Hebrews 4:6,14; 2 Peter 3:14
This is not talking about vision of the eyes. This is more about understanding God and His will so as to do what God wants us to do.

Seeking:
Matthew 6:33; Colossians 3:1-2
God and His righteousness; the things above. We must be seekers of righteousness. We must seek it, find it, and live it.

Separation:
2 Corinthians 6:17
Separate yourself from the world. No longer should you be considered a worldly person, but a spiritual one. Do not be like the world, and do not love the things of the world (1 John 2:15).

Servitude:
Romans 6:16-22; 2 Peter 2:16, 19; Romans 7:6; Galatians 5:13; Colossians 3:24; Romans 12:11
If there is any one word that should describe a Christian, it is this one. We are to be like Jesus, and He came in the form of a bondservant (Philippians 2:7). We should serve others. We should seek the better welfare of others. What better thing can we do for anyone than to share the gospel message with them? We are to do for others the things they can no longer do for themselves. We as Christians are servants of one another and our job is to serve one another by evangelism and edification.

Sincere:
1 Peter 2:2; Philippians 1:10; Titus 2:7
This is in relation to the heart (or mind). We must be sincere in our worship and service to God. Some teach that all one has to be is sincere and they can go to heaven. Can you read this list and believe such?

Sing:
1 Corinthians 14:15; Ephesians 5:19; Colossians 3:16
This is a command. We have no choice in the matter if we want to go to heaven. First, we should get enjoyment from our singing as we address God and give Him praise and glory. We should use this tool to teach others about Christ and how we are to live. We speak to each other to offer encouragement. Personally, I am frightened of the day when my voice can no longer offer praise to God. I think we should all feel this way.

Sober Minded:
Titus 2:6; Romans 12:3; 1 Thessalonians 5:6; 1 Peter 4:7: 1 Peter 5:8; 1 Timothy 2:9,15
As you can see, there are a lot of verses that command us to be sober minded or clear thinking people. Of course, this is in opposition to drunkenness or just plain old not thinking things out. We must live with a purpose in our lives and maintaining focus is the only way we are going to get there.

Sorrow:
2 Corinthians 2:3,7; 2 Corinthians 7:9,10
If we have sinned (and who has not?) we should have this sorrow. Sorrow to the point that we do not like to experience the pain of knowing we have disappointed God. We should grow to the point that we will not do the same sin again in our life. Sorrow helps us grow in a way.

Sound Doctrine:
Titus 1:9,13; Titus 2:1
Holding on to it and preaching it. Sound as compared to error and false teaching.

Sound Speech:
2 Timothy 1:13; Titus 2:8
This is like speaking as it were, the oracles of God (1 Peter 4:11). Whatever we teach and preach must be in accord with God's word. You cannot preach error or falsehood and still make it to heaven. If your teaching leads souls to hell, you are going there as well. Remember "Let the blind lead the blind, and both fall into the ditch"?

Sow to the Spirit:
Galatians 6:8
The context bears out that you reap what you sow. If you live your life seeking spiritual things you have a much better chance reaping spiritual life. If you live out of wonton pleasure and sin, you will reap corruption.

Speaking:
Ephesians 5:19; Ephesians 4;15; Ephesians 6:20; 1 Timothy 2:7
The idea here is communication. We speak to one another in singing. We speak to one another in love. We speak of our relationship with God and we guide others into the same kind of relationship.

Speech:
Colossians 4:6; Titus 2:8
This is the manner of our conversation and the condition of ourselves as we speak. The idea is that if you are going to preach God's word, you also need to live God's word in your life. Otherwise, people will call you a hypocrite and justly so. Do not give them such opportunity.

Sprinkled:
Hebrews 10:22
This is a reference to the Old Testament of cleansing. The sprinkling of blood upon the people was done as a purification process. That does not make sense to us in this day when we consider blood-borne pathogens and other diseases. But the fact that a sacrifice had been offered provided the justification before God. Our life is the sacrifice (Romans 12:1) that we offer to God, and in a way the blood of Jesus sprinkles us clean.

Stand:
1 Corinthians 15:1; Ephesians 6:11; Ephesians 6:13,14; 1 Peter 5:12
It has been said that if you will not stand for anything, you will fall for everything. Christians are told to make a decision and stick with it no matter what. The Christian is to stand firm (hold his/her place) without wavering. We also make a statement when we stand with the Lord and declare to the world our faith and conviction before God in any circumstance.

Stature:
Ephesians 4:13
The stature of Christ is what we are to develop ourselves into. The stature describes the entire person from their physical appearance to the character content of their life. We are to imitate the Christ and take on His stature.

Steadfastness:
1 Corinthians 7:37; 1 Corinthians 15:58; Hebrews 6:19; Colossians 2:5
Do not be like those who follow any doctrine that comes along. Find the truth and stick with it. It also means to be consistent in our speech and behavior so that we cannot be called a hypocrite by the adversaries of Jesus.

Stewardship:
1 Corinthians 9:17; Ephe3sians 3:2
We know that Paul was commissioned by Jesus to take the gospel to the Gentiles. In other words, Jesus put Paul in charge of the message of salvation. Paul took this commission seriously. In a way, we are entrusted with a duty to share the gospel message with others, just like Paul was entrusted to share the gospel with the Gentiles. If we do not respect this charge, we will not do it. But God has given this charge to all those who wear His name, and if we do not do it, we will not go to heaven.

Straight:
Matthew 7:14
Jesus said that those on the straight and narrow pathway leads to righteousness, and the broad way leads to destruction. Jesus also indicated that only a few would be on the narrow way. We have to make sure we live in such a way as to be on the narrow way.

Strength:
2 Corinthians 12:9; Mark 12:30,33; Luke 10:27; 1 Peter 5:10;Philippians 4:13
God and Christ are our strength. This thought is echoed in the Psalms many times. Yet we also understand that we need strength and integrity along with courage and determination to take a stand and fight against evil in all its forms. Joshua was told to be strong and courageous (Joshua 1:7).

Striving:
Philippians 1:27; Colossians 1:29; 2 Timothy 2:5
It seems as if we are in a constant battle. The evil one is always attacking us. Our journey through life is a constant struggle. We must always be striving to do what is right.

Study:
1 Timothy 2:15
How can one learn about God and His will without proper study? This study is more than attending Bible class and listening to the teacher. This is an effort on our part to learn how to properly handle the word of God. This can be done through topical or word studies. If possible, always enter your study period with prayer. Pray that your mind can be enlightened from the message from God.

Submit:
1 Corinthians 16:16; Ephesians 5:22-23; Colossians 3:18; James 4:7; 1 Peter 2:13; Ephesians 5:21
Submit to God by humbling yourself before Him. We do the same to Jesus by humbling ourselves before Him and keeping Him first in our lives. We also are commanded to submit to our brethren. We should treat our brethren as more important than ourselves (Philippians 2:3-4; Romans 12:10).

Sufferings:
Hebrews 5:8; Philippians 3:10; 1 Peter 4:13; Hebrews 5:8; Hebrews 2:10; 1 Peter 5:1
Suffering is never pleasant. Yet, there are times when it is good for us to suffer. Physical pain is not natural, and suffering pain tells your body that something is wrong. It is the suffering that moves us to seek medical assistance if possible. There are times when we consider that we are suffering for Christ. This should be a joyful occasion for us because we were able to stand strong in our faith as opposition stood against us.

Take Heed:
Matthew 6:1; Luke 8:8; 1 Corinthians 3:10; 1 Corinthians 8:9; 1 Corinthians 10:12; Colossians 4:17; Hebrews 3;12; 2 Peter 1:19
Beware, watch out, pay attention are just a few of the meanings here. We can become too confident in our faith; and such can lead to destruction. Remember that "pride goes before a fall" (Proverbs 16:18). We must also remember that Satan does not give up. He will try any method to make you stumble, so be very careful with your soul.

Tasted:
Hebrews 6:4,5
"O taste and see that the Lord is good.." (Psalm 34:8). The meaning in Psalm is to experience God on a personal level. This metaphor simply means to learn about God and all that He has done for us. This comes about by obedience. The passage in Hebrews is speaking of someone who became a Christian, yet turned away from God and Jesus sometime in their life. Our lesson should be that we should never give up in serving God. This is a lifetime endeavor on our part.

Temptation(resisting):
James 1:2; 1 Corinthians 10:13; James 1:12; 1 Peter 1:6
We all face it and if we can overcome it we will be better. This is one of the tools of Satan and Satan knows what tools to use in order to entrap us. There are different things used to tempt different people. What may not work on you might work on someone else. One person may be tempted by alcohol or drugs while another is tempted by greed. Whatever your temptation is, you must recognize it and know that the temptation does not come from God, but from Satan and your own mind (James 1:14).

Test:
1 John 4:1-6; 2 Corinthians 13:5; James 1:3
As we know the importance of sound teaching and keeping the church pure, we should pay attention to anyone who comes to bring a message our way. We must compare his teaching with the Bible. If his teaching is from God, it will become evident. We should examine ourselves on a regular basis. So, we test ourselves, we test preachers, we test our brethren, and we test the lost. We test them when we get them to examine their own condition before God.

Testify:
1 Peter 5:12; Acts 2:40
In a court of law, we stand up and testify to tell all the truth. Peter explains the letter written to those saints is his sworn testimony (the absolute truth). In a way we all need to testify of our faith in Jesus and we present evidence by our obedience.

Testimony:
2 Timothy 1:8
As we testify in a court of law, what we say is our testimony. As Christians, we affirm our faith in Jesus. We tell others what has happened. In our case, we are talking about what Jesus the Son of God did in the past. What we say is our testimony, and it needs to be the truth.

Thinking:
Romans 12:3; Philippians 4:8; 1 Corinthians 10:12
It is obvious that many people do not think about their actions and the consequences of their actions. Parents often marvel that their children did not think. They ask "what were you thinking" with a usual reply of "I don't know". Thinking should be coupled with sober-mindedness. As Christians we must consider our actions and possible consequences of our actions. A thought that should bother us is that if we do anything that might cause someone to question God or faith or the church because of my actions, and remain lost because of me. That bothers me, and I would imagine that we all have done something that if we had thought first and avoided whatever it was, we might have a few more Christians walking around.

Thirst:
2 Corinthians 11:27; Matthew 5:6; John 4:14; Romans 12:20
Our quest to learn God's word should be so strong that we can compare it to a person that is so thirsty, getting some water is the most important thing in their life. It becomes a matter of life and death to them. We should treat our quest to learn about God with a life and death mentality. It should be a top priority in our life.

Tradition:
Galatians 1:14; 2 Thessalonians 2:15
Some people despise traditions because they always want change. They do not like people telling them the truth, so they accuse those people of "holding to tradition". Paul commanded that the traditions that he practiced should be held onto. Doing things just because you have always done them becomes wrong unless you confirm through the scriptures that the actions are right to do. Romans 14:23 tells us that anything done without faith is sin. Doing things by tradition can be wrong if we do not compare them to the tradition given to us through the Bible.

Transformed:
Romans 12:2
Something is transformed when it is becomes different. When we in our sinful life change into the life commanded by God, we are transformed. Breaking down the word we see "trans" means across from or moving across things; and "formed" is something that is made. A little imagination and you see that Christians are "cross-made" people. Just because a person is baptized does not mean they have transformed anything; it is the evidence of the new life they now exhibit which shows the transformation in them.

Trust:
2 Corinthians 1:9,10; 1 Timothy 4:10; Ephesians 1:12-13
Trust is what your faith does for you. Rather than rely upon yourself to handle every situation you encounter, our faith leaves it all to God. Sure, there are things we must do for ourselves, but when it gets tough, we should rely upon God to handle our problems. The very middle verse of the Bible is Psalm 118:8 along with verse 9 which speaks of trusting in God over trusting in man or governments.

Truth:

John 1:14,17; John 8:32; John 4:21-24; Ephesians 4:15;1 Timothy 2:4; 1 Timothy 3:15; John 17:17

Jesus is the truth. God's word is the truth. We are to obey the truth. We are to practice the truth. We must realize that without the truth, we could never have known about God sending His Son to mankind. In every relationship we can think of on earth, truth has to be the foundation of such relationships. God gave us truth, and it is up to us to maintain the truth.

Turn:

1 Thessalonians 1:9

Can one be a Christian if they do not change their ways? No, we are to turn from our selfish ways to become obedient to Christ. Remember that the word translated "repentance" simple means to "change direction".

Unblameable:

Colossians 1:22; 1 Thessalonians 3:13

We must do everything we can to be without blame. We must behave so that others cannot blame us for unruly behavior. We must be an example of Christ as we interact with others. We are to be without spot or blemish and that means that no one can make a charge against us that will stick. This cannot happen if we continue in our sins.

Understanding:

Matthew 15:10; Hebrews 11:3; Acts 8:30; Ephesians 5:17; Philippians 4:7; Colossians 1:9;

This goes beyond just hearing something. It is taking what we have heard and learn the true meaning behind such words we hear. This goes to the why something was said and not merely the fact that something was said. This is where we make heads and tails of the matter. There is a purpose for everything God told us to do. Sometimes that purpose is hidden from our mind. But when we "get it", our mind is open and we can see mentally what it is all about.

Unfeigned:

2 Corinthians 6:6; 1 Timothy 1:5; 2 Timothy 1:5; 1 Peter 1:22

This word is translated in other versions as sincerity or being sincere.

Unity:

Ephesians 4:3,13

If you cannot get along with your brother, how can you get along with God? Unity is the agreement we have in our relationship. Being of the same mind means we all must learn what we should do and encourage everyone to do that in the same way. We must be intent on one purpose, which means we must view everything we do in the sense that we must help others get to heaven. Doing things together is much better than opposing each other. I think that in 1 John, the message is clear. If you cannot get along with your brethren, you cannot have a relationship with God. So, can't we all just get along?

Unmoveable:
1 Corinthians 15:58
Do not give up or give in. Hold your ground. Notice this is associated with steadfastness.

Unspotted:
James 1:27
The sacrifice to God needs to be without spot or blemish. In other words, pure. So we are to be before God. We can do this when we learn not to sin. Yet we still sin at various times. That is why we need to always be praying for forgiveness and God's continued blessings.

Virtue:
Philippians 4:8; 2 Peter 1:3,5
Moral Excellence as translated in the NASV. It means to be the best example of goodness that you can be which others can see and which also God witnesses in you.

Wait:
Romans 8:25; Galatians 5:5; 1 Thessalonians 5:10; 1 Corinthians 1:7
Sometimes wait means to hold your horses and give it time. Yet there is a sense in which we wait upon others. A waiter or waitress stand ready to serve you and see to your needs. We should be serving God and seeing to His desires. We do this by helping others get to heaven.

Walk, Walking:
Romans 6:4; 2 Corinthians 5:7; Galatians 6:16; Ephesians 2:10; Ephesians 4:1; Ephesians 5:5; Colossians 1:10; 1 John 1:7; 2 John 6; Galatians 5:16; Ephesians 5:2,8; Philippians 3:16
Rarely used in the sense of putting one foot in front of the other and moving in various directions. Most of the time in the New Testament, the word "walk" means our manner of life. Our behavior as we travel through life is our walk which becomes our lifestyle.

Warnings (Take Heed):
1 Thessalonians 5:14; Colossians1:28; Hebrews 3:12;1 Corinthians 10:12
There are so many warnings in the Bible, it is hard to imagine that people would not heed those warnings. We have warning signs all around and we recognize the danger associated with such warnings. But sadly, most people ignore the warnings from God which are designed to keep our souls in a saved condition. We would consider a person who ignored warnings to be a fool. Are we also not a fool to fail to respect the warnings from God?

Watch:

1 Corinthians 16;13; 1 Thessalonians 5:6; 2 Timothy 4:5; Revelation 3:2

Everything we do should be done with the mindset that Jesus is returning someday, and when that day is continues to be a mystery because only God knows that time. So Jesus and the disciples teach us to be ready at any moment or be ready all the time. If our heart is set on spiritual things, we are watching for the Lord to return.

Water:

Acts 8:36; John 3:5; Ephesians 5:26

Water plays an important role in our salvation. 1 Peter 3:21-22 explains this very well. It is not the cleaning of the body, but a conscious effort to appeal to God that as we call on Him, and do what He commanded, we can have our sins washed away by the water. Water by itself does not save. But, when we through faith are baptized in water, our sins are washed away.

Weakness:

1 Corinthians 1:25; 2 Corinthians 12:9

Not by being weak, but acknowledging our weakness. This is very similar to humility.

Willingly:

1 Peter 5:2

We have to make the choice to serve God from the heart. If we do so by compulsion, there is no choice in the matter. We should want to serve God, not feel forced to serve Him.

Wisdom:

Ephesians 1:8; Ephesians 3:10; Ephesians 4:5; James 1:5; Ephesians 5:15; 2 Timothy 3:15

The application of the knowledge coupled with the knowledge of what God wants us to be. When we do this, we are considered wise.

Withdraw:

2 Thessalonians 3:6; 1 Timothy 6:5

2 Corinthians 6:14-18 expresses that we should withdraw from every form of evil, every person that is unruly, and those who reject Christ. Isaiah 52:11 tells us to come out from their midst. Sin is compared to a cancer, and as the physical body needs to rid itself from cancer to live, so we must also rid ourselves of sin and the influences that cause us to sin.

Witness:

Acts 4:33; 2 Timothy 2:2

We must share the gospel message and do those things that the early church did. There are times when we can offer testimony about our feelings and what God has done for us. None of us were witnesses of the Christ, but we are those whom the Lord spoke of who would believe because of the word spoken by them (John 17:20).

Words:
Matthew 12:37
Watch what you say, for your words can impact your destiny.

Works:
James 2:14-26; Revelation 2:26; Romans 8:28; Philippians 2:12;Hebrews 6:10;
Romans 2:10
There are no works of righteousness which we can do ourselves. But when we do the works God has commanded us, we are doing His will, and He is pleased with our actions. Our works are to be seen by others (Matthew 5:16), and that is what we are created in Christ Jesus for (Ephesians 2:10).

Worship:
John 4:24; Philippians 3:3
Some say that all of life is worship, yet we must qualify that statement. Our worship towards God should be our number one priority. Trying to please God must be our goal. Giving God the honor due His name is the reason He created man in the first place. We must worship in spirit which is the emotional feelings we have towards God, yet we must also worship in truth according to His instructions and the examples we have from the New Testament.

Worthy:
Luke 3:8; Ephesians 4:1; Colossians 1:10; 1 Timothy 1:15;
We must be worthy of the Lord to gain His approval. Thus, we must meet certain requirements. Obedience of the gospel and continued faithfulness puts us in this condition. Only those who have done this will get to heaven.

Yield:
Romans 6:13,16,19; Hebrews 12:11
We must give in or yield to God. This is the action that is caused by humility.

Zeal:
2 Corinthians 7:11; 2 Corinthians 9:2; Philippians 3:6; Colossians 4:13; Titus 2:14
Does anyone actually believe that one can go to heaven if they do not have zeal? This is one of the most endearing qualities of those in the first century.

I hope you realize that some of these things could have had an entire chapter dedicated to them.

If you study all the things recorded in the above lists, you will realize this all comes from God through the Holy Spirits workings. These things are right. All of them are. If we are not trying to grow these things into our lives it could be sin; and remember that sin keeps us out of heaven.

We have not looked at the "thou shalt not's" and the various list from the scriptures that will keep one out of heaven. We have not discussed the works of the flesh from Galatians 5:19-21 or the list of sins the Corinthians had been involved in before their conversion which we find in 1 Corinthians 6:9-10. We did not discuss the things of the old self from Colossians 3:5-11.

Yes there are a lot of negative commands, and there are multiple warnings to take heed lest you fall (1 Corinthians 10:12). We have many warnings about being deceived. If we concentrate on doing the good things of the list, we will not need to worry about losing our soul (Philippians 4:8). Yet if we turn to false teaching or depart from the Lord, we cannot be saved.

Remember to "grow in the grace and knowledge of our Lord and Savior, Jesus Christ." (2 Peter 3:18). That is why we have to make the salvation of our soul a lifelong effort and work hard to please God in all things. Jesus said in His prayer: "Not my will, but Thy will be done". When we can make that our motto, we are on the right path.

As we wrap things up here, let me offer one last verse to consider. "Therefore, to one who knows the right thing to do, and does not do it, to him it is sin" (James 4:17 NASV). May God bless you as you seek to obtain the salvation that He offers through His Son.

Carey Scott currently resides in Ranger Texas. He is the webmaster for the site www.simplebiblestudies.com

Made in the USA
Las Vegas, NV
09 October 2021